CHICAGO COOKBOOK

TASTE THE WINDY CITY WITH EASY CHICAGO RECIPES

By
BookSumo Press
Copyright © by Saxonberg Associates

Published by
BookSumo Press, a DBA of Saxonberg Associates
http://www.booksumo.com/

ABOUT THE AUTHOR.

BookSumo Press is a publisher of unique, easy, and healthy cookbooks.

Our cookbooks span all topics and all subjects. If you want a deep dive into the possibilities of cooking with any type of ingredient. Then BookSumo Press is your go to place for robust yet simple and delicious cookbooks and recipes. Whether you are looking for great tasting pressure cooker recipes or authentic ethic and cultural food. BookSumo Press has a delicious and easy cookbook for you.

With simple ingredients, and even simpler step-by-step instructions BookSumo cookbooks get everyone in the kitchen chefing delicious meals.

BookSumo is an independent publisher of books operating in the beautiful Garden State (NJ) and our team of chefs and kitchen experts are here to teach, eat, and be merry!

INTRODUCTION

Welcome to *The Effortless Chef Series*! Thank you for taking the time to purchase this cookbook.

Come take a journey into the delights of easy cooking. The point of this cookbook and all BookSumo Press cookbooks is to exemplify the effortless nature of cooking simply.

In this book we focus on Chicago cooking. You will find that even though the recipes are simple, the taste of the dishes are quite amazing.

So will you take an adventure in simple cooking? If the answer is yes please consult the table of contents to find the dishes you are most interested in.

Once you are ready, jump right in and start cooking.

— BookSumo Press

TABLE OF CONTENTS

About the Author...2

Introduction 3

Table of Contents 4

Any Issues? Contact Us 9

Legal Notes..10

Common Abbreviations...11

Chapter 1: Easy Chicago Recipes 12

    Plantain Steak Sandwich..12

    Hummus Rice Bake...15

    Chicago Chick-anoff...17

    Worcestershire Fondue 19

    Crunchy Broccoli Salad 21

    Dublin Casserole 23

    Broccoli Fries 25

    Sloppy Joe's Chicago...27

    Tuesday's Casserole 29

    Chicago Chicken Cutlets..31

    Midway Minestrone 33

    Ranch Wontons 36

Pesto Florets Salad...38

Basmati Hearts Rice...40

Lovers' Red Wine Stew...42

BBQ Chicken Tots...44

Scaloppini Duck...46

Autumn Mushroom Bake...48

Ginger Ale Stew...50

Picante Slow Cooker...52

Chicago Dump Cake...54

Monday's Ground Beef Macaroni Bake................................56

Potato Pot Gratin...58

Carol's Chocolate Cake...60

Smoked Potato and Sausage Gratin.....................................62

Velveeta Casserole...64

4-Ingredient Pot Roast...66

Spicy Garbanzo and Turkey Stew...68

Paseo Tilapia with Salsa...70

Chicken Bop Dip..72

Quick Pot Cake..74

Chicago Roast Dump Dinner...76

Pearls Stir Fry...78

Golden Chicken Breasts with Shallot Salsa..........................80

Perfect Pasta Salad..82

Latin Veggies Casserole..84

Rotini Turkey Stew..86

Chicago Breakfast Pitas...89

Teriyaki Wontons...91

Condensed Macaroni Bake..93

Chicken Rice with Cheddar Sauce 96

Chicago Black Bean and Cream Wraps...98

Homemade Blueberry Blintzes 101

Classic Chicken and Broccoli Casserole......................................104

Bell Beef and Rice Soup 106

Chunky and Cheesy Taco Dip...108

Red Potatoes and Root Vegetables 110

How to Make a Hot Dog Chicago Style.......................................112

Dempster Dip..114

Pizza Skillet..116

Deep Dish Dough 118

Six Corners Pizza..120

Chicago City Chili...123

Full Macaroni Salad 125

Italian Beef Lunch...128

Chicago Restaurant Duck..131

Chicago Cub's Italian Dip...133

Ballpark Salmon..135

Full Italian Beef 137

Maria's Italian Beef 140

Italian Beef II 142

Squash and Steaks in the Pressure Cooker 144

Italian Pizza Minis 147

West Town Spicy Relish 149

Depaul Glazed Meatballs...151

Oatmeal Chocolate Cookies 153

Shrimp Casserole 155

Egg Salad Chicago 157

Chicken with White Glaze 159

Chicago Burgers with Pepper Aioli....................................161

Illinois Chowder..164

Vanilla Cheesecakes 166

Provolone Chicken Hoagies 168

Alternative Hot Dogs Chicago Style 170

Simple Italian Beef..172

How to Make Beef Au Jus 174

(Roasted Beef Sauce) 174

Motel Pizza..176

Illinois Sweet Savory Chili...179

Classic Ritz Chicken Bake 182

Cloud Gate Pizza Sauce 184

Simple Vanilla Cookies..186

Frankfurter Salad Chi-Town Style.....................................188

Alternative Deep Dish 190

Coffee Cakes 101..193

Chicago Tuna Salad..196

Amaretto Raisins Cookies 198

Garlic Dough for Thin Crusts 201

Homemade Deep Dish 203

Blue Sirloin Steak.. 206

Simple Garlic Pizza Crust 208

Italian Style Grilled Chicken 210

Downtown Ribs... 212

How to Make Sausages.. 215

THANKS FOR READING! JOIN THE CLUB AND KEEP ON COOKING WITH 6
MORE COOKBOOKS.... 217

Come On... 219

Let's Be Friends :).. 219

Any Issues? Contact Us

If you find that something important to you is missing from this book please contact us at info@booksumo.com.

We will take your concerns into consideration when the 2nd edition of this book is published. And we will keep you updated!

— BookSumo Press

LEGAL NOTES

COMMON ABBREVIATIONS

cup(s)	C.
tablespoon	tbsp
teaspoon	tsp
ounce	oz.
pound	lb

*All units used are standard American measurements

Chapter 1: Easy Chicago Recipes

Plantain Steak Sandwich

Ingredients

- 2 C. vegetable oil for frying
- 1 green plantain, peeled and halved lengthwise
- 2 tbsp vegetable oil
- 1 clove garlic, minced
- 4 oz beef skirt steak, cut into thin strips
- 1/4 medium yellow onion, thinly sliced
- 1 pinch cumin
- 1 pinch dried oregano
- 1 tbsp mayonnaise
- 1 slice processed American cheese, cut in half
- 2 slices tomato
- 3 leaves lettuce

Directions

- Place a large pan over medium heat. Heat 2 C. of oil in it. Cook in it the plantains for 2 to 3 min or until they become golden.
- Drain the plantains and place them on a board. Use a rolling pin or the back of a skillet to flatten them.
- Place them back in the hot oil and cook them for another 3 min and become golden brown. Drain them and place them aside.

- Place a large pan over medium heat. Heat in it 2 tbsp of oil. Sauté in it the garlic, skirt steak, onion, cumin and oregano for 8 min while stirring often.
- Use a knife to spread the mayo over the fried plantains and place one of them on a serving plate.
- Lay over it the cheese with steak mixture, lettuce, and tomato. Cover them with the second half of the plantain then serve it.
- Enjoy.

Servings Per Recipe: 1

Timing Information:

Preparation	10 m
Cooking	15 m
Total Time	25 m

Nutritional Information:

Calories	1219 kcal
Fat	100.4 g
Carbohydrates	65.4g
Protein	23.6 g
Cholesterol	68 mg
Sodium	551 mg

* Percent Daily Values are based on a 2,000 calorie diet.

HUMMUS RICE BAKE

Ingredients

- 2 (15 -22 1/2 oz) cans chickpeas, drained and rinsed
- 3 -4 C. cooked brown rice
- 1 (28 oz) cans diced tomatoes, undrained
- 1 medium white onion, chopped
- 1 tsp garlic powder
- 1 tsp dried oregano
- 1 tsp dried basil
- 1 -2 tsp dried parsley
- 3 tbsp tahini
- 3 tbsp water
- 1 tbsp toasted sesame seeds (optional)

Directions

- Before you do anything, preheat the oven to 375 F. Grease a casserole dish with some olive oil.
- Get a mixing bowl: Whisk in it the water with the tahini.
- Combine the remaining ingredients in the casserole dish well. Season them with a pinch of salt and pepper.
- Spread over it the tahini and water mix. Place it the oven and cook it for 42 min.
- Top the rice casserole with some sesame seeds then cook them in the oven for an extra 4 min. Serve it warm.
- Enjoy.

Servings Per Recipe: 6

Timing Information:

Preparation	10 mins
Total Time	55 mins

Nutritional Information:

Calories	354.4
Fat	6.3g
Cholesterol	0.0mg
Sodium	438.7mg
Carbohydrates	64.3g
Protein	12.1g

* Percent Daily Values are based on a 2,000 calorie diet.

CHICAGO CHICK-ANOFF

Ingredients

- 1 lb boneless skinless chicken breast, frozen
- 1 (10 1/2 oz) cans cream of mushroom soup, undiluted
- 16 oz sour cream
- 1 (1 oz) package onion soup mix

Directions

- Grease a slow cooker with some butter. Lay in it the chicken breasts then season them with some salt and pepper.
- Get a mixing bowl: Whisk in it the soup mix with mushroom soup and sour cream. Pour it over the chicken breasts.
- Put on the lid and let them cook for 8 h on low. Serve your creamy chicken with some rice.
- Enjoy.

Servings Per Recipe: 6

Timing Information:

| Preparation | 5 mins |
| Total Time | 8 hrs 5 mins |

Nutritional Information:

Calories	296.1
Fat	20.6g
Cholesterol	89.8mg
Sodium	879.3mg
Carbohydrates	8.7g
Protein	18.8g

* Percent Daily Values are based on a 2,000 calorie diet.

WORCESTERSHIRE FONDUE

Ingredients

- 4 oz broth
- 1 tsp chopped garlic
- 6 oz cheddar cheese
- pepper
- mustard powder, garnish
- Worcestershire sauce, garnish
- apple, for dipping

Directions

- Place a heavy saucepan over medium heat. Stir in it the broth with milk and heat them through.
- Add the remaining ingredients and mix them well until they cheese melts. Serve your fondue hot.
- Enjoy.

Servings Per Recipe: 3

Timing Information:

Preparation	15 mins
Total Time	15 mins

Nutritional Information:

Calories	247.3
Fat	18.8g
Cholesterol	59.6mg
Sodium	354.4mg
Carbohydrates	2.4g
Protein	14.3g

* Percent Daily Values are based on a 2,000 calorie diet.

CRUNCHY BROCCOLI SALAD

Ingredients

- 2 bunches broccoli, trimmed
- 1/2 C. balsamic vinegar
- 1/2 C. butter
- 2 tbsp firmly packed brown sugar
- 1/4 tsp salt
- 1/4 tsp ground black pepper

Directions

- Place the broccoli in a steamer and let it cook for 8 to 10 min.
- Place a heavy saucepan over medium heat. Stir in it the balsamic vinaigrette and let it cook until half it evaporates.
- Add the butter, brown sugar, salt and pepper then whisk them until they become smooth.
- Get a large mixing bowl: Toss in it the broccoli with the dressing then serve it right away.
- Enjoy.

Servings Per Recipe: 6

Timing Information:

Preparation	10 mins
Total Time	20 mins

Nutritional Information:

Calories	240.9
Fat	16.1g
Cholesterol	40.6mg
Sodium	305.0mg
Carbohydrates	21.6g
Protein	6.0g

* Percent Daily Values are based on a 2,000 calorie diet.

DUBLIN CASSEROLE

Ingredients

- 4 C. chopped cabbage
- 1 C. sliced celery
- 1/2 C. chopped onion
- 1/4 C. butter
- 8 oz pasta, cooked, drained
- 1 (12 oz) cans corned beef
- 4 oz shredded swiss cheese
- 1/2 C. milk
- 1/2 tsp dry mustard
- 1/2 tsp caraway seed
- 1/4 tsp pepper

Directions

- Before you do anything, preheat the oven to 350 F.
- Place a large skillet over medium heat. Melt in it the butter. Cook in it the cabbage, celery and onion for 8 min.
- Transfer the mix to a greased baking dish. Stir in the rest of the ingredients and mix them well.
- Cover the pan with a piece of foil and cook it in the oven for 48 min. Serve your corned pasta casserole hot.
- Enjoy.

Servings Per Recipe: 8

Timing Information:

Preparation	20 mins
Total Time	1 hr 10 mins

Nutritional Information:

Calories	343.0
Fat	18.8g
Cholesterol	72.1mg
Sodium	585.9mg
Carbohydrates	26.4g
Protein	16.5g

* Percent Daily Values are based on a 2,000 calorie diet.

BROCCOLI FRIES

Ingredients

- broccoli
- butter
- parmesan cheese, to taste

Directions

- Bring a large salted pot of water to a boil. Cook in it the broccoli for 7 min.
- Place the a large pan over medium heat.
- Drain the broccoli from the water. Toss in a large mixing bowl with the parmesan cheese.
- Cook the broccoli florets in the hot oil for 3 to 5 min. Serve it warm with your favorite dip.
- Enjoy.

Servings Per Recipe: 6

Timing Information:

Preparation	20 mins
Total Time	40 mins

Nutritional Information:

Calories	0.0
Fat	0.0g
Cholesterol	0.0mg
Sodium	0.0mg
Carbohydrates	0.0g
Protein	0.0g

* Percent Daily Values are based on a 2,000 calorie diet.

Sloppy Joe's Chicago

Ingredients

- 2 lbs ground beef
- 3 large onions, diced
- 2 large green peppers, diced
- 1/2 C. barbecue sauce
- 2 tbsp Worcestershire sauce
- 1 1/2 tsp mustard
- 1 tbsp sugar
- 3 tbsp vinegar
- 1 1/2 tsp salt
- 20 oz catsup

Directions

- Place a large pot over medium heat. Cook in it the beef for 10 min over medium high heat.
- Discard the excess fat. Add to it the remaining ingredients and put on the lid. Let them cook for 1 h 45 min over low heat.
- Spoon the mix into buns then serve them hot.
- Enjoy.

Servings Per Recipe: 8

Timing Information:

Preparation	20 mins
Total Time	1 hr 20 mins

Nutritional Information:

Calories	367.2
Fat	77.1mg
Cholesterol	1489.1mg
Sodium	29.9g
Carbohydrates	23.5g
Protein	367.2

* Percent Daily Values are based on a 2,000 calorie diet.

TUESDAY'S CASSEROLE

Ingredients

- 1 (14 3/4 oz) cans creamed corn
- 1 (15 1/4 oz) cans whole corn, drained
- 1 C. melted butter
- 3 eggs
- 1 C. sour cream
- 1 tbsp sugar
- 1 (8 1/2 oz) boxes Jiffy corn muffin mix

Directions

- Before you do anything, preheat the oven to 350 F.
- Drain the corn and combine it with the remaining ingredients in a greased casserole dish.
- Place it in the fridge and cook it for 64 min. Serve it hot.
- Enjoy.

Servings Per Recipe: 6

Timing Information:

Preparation	15 mins
Total Time	1 hr 15 mins

Nutritional Information:

Calories	673.6
Fat	46.8g
Cholesterol	195.0mg
Sodium	891.0mg
Carbohydrates	58.5g
Protein	10.7g

* Percent Daily Values are based on a 2,000 calorie diet.

CHICAGO CHICKEN CUTLETS

Ingredients

- 5 -6 chicken breasts
- corn flake crumbs
- 2 eggs
- flour

Directions

- Before you do anything, preheat the oven to 350 F.
- Place the chicken breasts between 2 pieces of parchment papers. Use a kitchen hammer to flatten them. Season them with some salt and pepper.
- Beat 2 eggs in a shallow bowl. Spread each of the flour and corn flakes crumbs on a separate shallow bowls.
- Dust the chicken breasts with flour then dip them in the beaten eggs and coat them with the corn flakes.
- Place the chicken breasts on a baking pan. Cook them in the oven for 48 min. Serve your chicken breasts warm.
- Enjoy.

Servings Per Recipe: 6

Timing Information:

Preparation	20 mins
Total Time	1 hr 5 mins

Nutritional Information:

Calories	207.8
Fat	11.1g
Cholesterol	77.3mg
Sodium	76.1mg
Carbohydrates	0.0g
Protein	25.1g

* Percent Daily Values are based on a 2,000 calorie diet.

MIDWAY MINESTRONE

Ingredients

- 1/4 lb fresh green beans, trimmed and cut into 1 inch pieces
- 2 medium zucchini, trimmed and cut into 1/2 inch dices
- 1 large potato, peeled and cut into 3/4 inch dices
- 1/2 lb cabbage, roughly chopped
- 1/3 C. olive oil
- 3 tbsp butter
- 2 medium onions, chopped
- 3 medium carrots, coarsely chopped
- 3 celery ribs, coarsely chopped
- 2 garlic cloves, minced
- 1 (28 oz) cans Italian plum tomatoes, undrained and chopped
- 3 1/2 C. beef broth
- 1 1/2 C. water
- 1/2 tsp salt
- 1/2 tsp dried basil leaves, crushed
- 1/4 tsp dried rosemary leaves, crushed
- 1/4 tsp fresh black pepper
- 1 bay leaf
- 1 (16 oz) cans cannellini beans
- freshly grated parmesan cheese (optional)

Directions

- Place a large pot over medium heat. Melt the butter with oil in it. Sauté in it the onion for 7 min.

- Add the carrots with potato and let them cook for 6 min. Add the celery with beans and let them cook for another 6 min.
- Add the zucchini and cook them for an extra 4 min. Add the garlic with cabbage then let them cook for 2 min while stirring all the time.
- Stir in the broth, water and tomato with its juice, basil, rosemary, bay leaf, a pinch of salt and pepper. Cook them until they start boiling.
- Lower the heat and put on the lid. Cook the stew for 1 h 35 min while stirring from time to time.
- Once the time is up, drain the canned beans and add it to the pot with the green beans. Cook the stew for an extra 38 min without a lid.
- Discard the bay leaf then serve your stew hot.
- Enjoy

Servings Per Recipe: 8

Timing Information:

| Preparation | 20 mins |
| Total Time | 2 hrs 20 mins |

Nutritional Information:

Calories	301.3
Fat	14.3g
Cholesterol	11.4mg
Sodium	625.5mg
Carbohydrates	35.9g
Protein	10.4g

* Percent Daily Values are based on a 2,000 calorie diet.

RANCH WONTONS

Ingredients

- 1 lb bulk breakfast sausage, browned, rinsed and drained.
- 3/4 C. ranch dressing
- 1/4 C. mayonnaise
- 1 C. shredded Monterey jack pepper cheese
- 1 C. shredded Monterey jack cheese
- 50 wonton wrappers

Directions

- Before you do anything, preheat the oven to 350 F.
- Grease a muffin tin with a cooking spray. Press in it the wonton wrappers to make them in the shape of C..
- Place the pan in the oven and cook it for 5 min then place them aside.
- Get a large mixing bowl: Combine in it the remaining ingredients and mix them well. Divide the filling between the wonton C..
- Place the tin back in the oven and cook them for 4 min then serve them hot.
- Enjoy.

Servings Per Recipe: 1

Timing Information:

Preparation	10 mins
Total Time	20 mins

Nutritional Information:

Calories	93.2
Fat	6.3g
Cholesterol	13.6mg
Sodium	180.8mg
Carbohydrates	5.1g
Protein	3.7g

* Percent Daily Values are based on a 2,000 calorie diet.

PESTO FLORETS SALAD

Ingredients

- 10 oz basil pesto
- 1 lb penne pasta
- 1 lb broccoli, cut into small florets
- 2 (6 oz) tyson grilled chicken breast strips
- 3 oz shredded parmesan cheese

Directions

- Slice the broccoli into florets. Place it aside.
- Cook the pasta according to the directions on the package for 3 min only. Stir in the broccoli florets and cook them for 4 min.
- Drain the broccoli and pasta from the water. Place the chicken pieces in the pot and cook them for 2 to 3 min to heat them through.
- Drain the chicken from the water.
- Get a large mixing bowl: Combine it the broccoli with chicken, pasta, cheese, pesto sauce, a pinch of salt and pepper. Toss them to coat. Serve it right away.
- Enjoy.

Servings Per Recipe: 4

Timing Information:

Preparation	15 mins
Total Time	25 mins

Nutritional Information:

Calories	856.8
Fat	14.7g
Cholesterol	91.0mg
Sodium	453.2mg
Carbohydrates	142.3g
Protein	56.5g

* Percent Daily Values are based on a 2,000 calorie diet.

BASMATI HEARTS RICE

Ingredients

- 1/4 C. olive oil
- 1 medium onions
- 1 medium red bell peppers
- 6 garlic cloves, crushed
- 2 C. brown basmati rice
- 1 lemons, juiced
- 3 C. vegetable broth
- 1 tsp salt
- 1 tsp black pepper
- 1 (14 oz) cans artichoke hearts, drained, cut into quarters
- 2 (15 oz) cans chickpeas, drained
- 6 tbsp parmesan cheese

Directions

- Place a large skillet over medium heat. Heat the olive oil in it.
- Cook in it the rice for 3 min. Stir in the bell pepper with onion for 4 min.
- Stir in the garlic and cook them for another minute. Add the broth, lemon juice, salt and pepper. Cook them until they start boiling.
- Put on the lid and cook the rice for 42 min over low heat. Add the artichokes and chickpeas to the pot.
- Put on the lid and cook them for an extra 6 min. Serve your rice hot with some parmesan cheese.
- Enjoy.

Servings Per Recipe: 6

Timing Information:

Preparation	30 mins
Total Time	1 hr 30 mins

Nutritional Information:

Calories	592.2
Fat	15.0g
Cholesterol	5.6mg
Sodium	1517.9mg
Carbohydrates	98.8g
Protein	18.2g

* Percent Daily Values are based on a 2,000 calorie diet.

LOVERS' RED WINE STEW

Ingredients

- 2 lbs beef stew meat, cut in 1 1/2 inch chunks
- 2 medium onions, quartered
- 3 stalks celery, cut in large chunks
- 4 carrots, cut in 1 1/2 inch pieces
- 2 large potatoes, cut in 1 1/2 inch pieces
- 1 C. tomato juice
- 1/4 C. tapioca
- 1 tbsp sugar
- 1 tbsp salt
- 1/4 tsp pepper
- 1/2 tsp dried basil
- 1/2 C. dry red wine
- 1/2 C. water

Directions

- Before you do anything, preheat the oven to 300 F.
- Place a large pot over medium heat. Combine all the ingredients except for the potato. Put on the lid and let them cook for 3 h over low heat.
- Once the time is up, stir in the potato. Cook the stew for an extra 60 min.
- Serve your stew hot with some rice.
- Enjoy.

Servings Per Recipe: 6

Timing Information:

Preparation	15 mins
Total Time	4 hrs 15 mins

Nutritional Information:

Calories	706.4
Fat	39.1g
Cholesterol	157.3mg
Sodium	1422.3mg
Carbohydrates	39.7g
Protein	43.9g

* Percent Daily Values are based on a 2,000 calorie diet.

BBQ Chicken Tots

Ingredients

- 1 egg
- 2 tbsp milk
- 4 C. barbecue potato chips, crushed
- 1/2 lb boneless skinless chicken breast, cut into 1 1/2 inch cubes
- barbecue sauce

Directions

- Before you do anything, preheat the oven to 400 F.
- Mix the milk with egg in a shallow plate.
- Spread the potato chips in a shallow plate.
- Coat the chicken breasts with the eggs mix then cover them with the potato chips.
- Lay the chicken breasts on a cookie sheet. Cook them in the oven for 14 to 16 min then serve them warm.
- Enjoy.

Servings Per Recipe: 4

Timing Information:

Preparation	10 mins
Total Time	25 mins

Nutritional Information:

Calories	85.6
Fat	2.2g
Cholesterol	86.8mg
Sodium	58.1mg
Carbohydrates	0.4g
Protein	14.9g

* Percent Daily Values are based on a 2,000 calorie diet.

SCALOPPINI DUCK

Ingredients

- 1 C. buckwheat flour
- 4 tbsp honey
- 4 boneless skinless duck breasts
- 4 C. cooked brown rice
- 1 C. buttermilk

Directions

- Before you do anything, preheat the oven to 350 F.
- Flatten the duck breasts with a hammer or pan.
- Lay 1 tbsp of honey over each breasts. Place them in the buttermilk then drain them and coat them with the buckwheat flour.
- Lay the duck breasts on a lined up cookie sheet. Cook them in the oven for 35 min. Serve your honey duck breasts warm.
- Enjoy.

Servings Per Recipe: 4

Timing Information:

| Preparation | 20 mins |
| Total Time | 50 mins |

Nutritional Information:

Calories	540.2
Fat	5.4g
Cholesterol	138.3mg
Sodium	170.1mg
Carbohydrates	87.2g
Protein	36.6g

* Percent Daily Values are based on a 2,000 calorie diet.

AUTUMN MUSHROOM BAKE

Ingredients

- 2 C. uncooked rice
- 2 (10 1/2 oz) cans chicken broth
- 10 1/2 fluid oz water
- 1/2 C. butter
- 12 oz canned mushrooms
- 1 tsp salt
- 1 medium onion, chopped

Directions

- Before you do anything, preheat the oven to 350 F.
- Get a baking pan and grease it with some butter. Combine in it all the ingredients and mix them well.
- Place the pan in the oven and cook it for 60 min. Serve it hot.
- Enjoy.

Servings Per Recipe: 8

Timing Information:

Preparation	15 mins
Total Time	1 hr 15 mins

Nutritional Information:

Calories	309.9
Fat	12.5g
Cholesterol	30.5mg
Sodium	811.8mg
Carbohydrates	42.3g
Protein	6.8g

* Percent Daily Values are based on a 2,000 calorie diet.

GINGER ALE STEW

Ingredients

- 1 lb beef stew meat
- 1 can cream of mushroom soup, undiluted
- 1 package onion and mushroom soup mix
- 1/2 C. ginger ale soda
- 3 (4 oz) cans mushroom pieces

Directions

- Combine the mushroom soup, mushroom/onion soup, mushrooms and ginger ale in a slow cooker.
- Stir into it the stew meat with a pinch of salt and pepper. Put on the lid and let them cook for 6 h on low.
- Serve your stew warm with some noodles or rice.
- Enjoy.

Servings Per Recipe: 4

Timing Information:

Preparation	10 mins
Total Time	6 hrs 10 mins

Nutritional Information:

Calories	238.6
Fat	9.8g
Cholesterol	72.5mg
Sodium	628.8mg
Carbohydrates	10.7g
Protein	28.5g

* Percent Daily Values are based on a 2,000 calorie diet.

PICANTE SLOW COOKER

Ingredients

- 3 -4 chicken breasts
- 1 jar picante sauce

Directions

- Place the chicken breasts in a greased slow cooker. Pour the sauce all over it.
- Put on the lid and let it cook for 6 h. Serve your saucy chicken hot.
- Enjoy.

Servings Per Recipe: 6

Timing Information:

Preparation	5 mins
Total Time	6 hrs 5 mins

Nutritional Information:

Calories	124.7
Fat	6.7g
Cholesterol	46.4mg
Sodium	45.6mg
Carbohydrates	0.0g
Protein	15.1g

* Percent Daily Values are based on a 2,000 calorie diet.

CHICAGO DUMP CAKE

Ingredients

- 1 (18 1/4 oz) boxes spice cake mix
- 2 (21 oz) cans apple pie filling
- 1 tsp ground cinnamon
- 1 tsp ground nutmeg
- 1 tsp ground allspice
- 1 tbsp granulated sugar
- 3/4 C. butter
- 1 C. chopped nuts

Directions

- Before you do anything, preheat the oven to 350 F. Grease a casserole dish with some butter.
- Get a small mixing bowl: Stir in it the cinnamon, nutmeg, allspice and sugar.
- Spread the apple pie filling in the casserole dish. Top it with the spice mix followed by the cake mix.
- Sprinkle the nuts with butter on top. Place the pan in the oven and cook it for 1 h.
- Serve your pudding cake with some ice cream.
- Enjoy.

Servings Per Recipe: 12

Timing Information:

Preparation	10 mins
Total Time	55 mins

Nutritional Information:

Calories	464.8
Fat	23.5g
Cholesterol	30.5mg
Sodium	485.5mg
Carbohydrates	62.6g
Protein	4.1g

* Percent Daily Values are based on a 2,000 calorie diet.

MONDAY'S GROUND BEEF MACARONI BAKE

Ingredients

- 1 box Kraft macaroni and cheese
- 1 (10 oz) cans cream of mushroom soup
- 1 lb ground beef
- 1 (4 oz) cans mushrooms
- 1/4 chopped onion
- salt
- pepper
- milk, 1 soup can full

Directions

- Before you do anything, preheat the oven to 350 F.
- Cook the macaroni according to the directions on the package.
- In the meantime, place a large skillet over medium heat. Cook in it the beef with onion for 8 min.
- Get a baking pan and coat it with some butter. Combine in it the cooked beef with mushrooms, cream of mushroom soup, and 1 can of milk.
- Stir into them the cheese with cooked macaroni, a pinch of salt and pepper.
- Place the pan in the oven and cook it for 40 to 48 min. Serve it hot.
- Enjoy.

Servings Per Recipe: 6

Timing Information:

Preparation	20 mins
Total Time	1 hr 5 mins

Nutritional Information:

Calories	206.8
Fat	14.1g
Cholesterol	51.4mg
Sodium	355.8mg
Carbohydrates	3.8g
Protein	15.4g

* Percent Daily Values are based on a 2,000 calorie diet.

POTATO POT GRATIN

Ingredients

- 1 (32 oz) packages frozen hash brown potatoes
- 2 (10 oz) cans cheddar cheese soup, undiluted
- 1 (13 oz) cans evaporated milk, undiluted
- 1 (3 oz) cans French fried onion rings, divided
- salt and pepper

Directions

- Grease a slow cooker with some butter. Place 1/4 C. of onion rings aside.
- Toss in it the potatoes, soup, milk, the remaining onion rings, a pinch of salt and pepper.
- Put on the lid and let them cook for 8 h on low. Serve your potato gratin with the remaining onion rings then serve it hot.
- Enjoy.

Servings Per Recipe: 8

Timing Information:

Preparation	10 mins
Total Time	8 hrs 10 mins

Nutritional Information:

Calories	240.4
Fat	9.9g
Cholesterol	29.6mg
Sodium	603.4mg
Carbohydrates	30.5g
Protein	8.4g

* Percent Daily Values are based on a 2,000 calorie diet.

CAROL'S CHOCOLATE CAKE

Ingredients

- 1 (18 oz) boxes chocolate cake mix
- 1 C. warm water, divided
- 3 tbsp oil
- 2 eggs
- 1/3 C. chopped nuts (optional)
- 1/4 C. chocolate syrup
- 3 tbsp sugar

Directions

- Get a large mixing bowl: Whisk in it the cake mix, 3/4 C. water, oil and eggs. Fold into it the nuts.
- Pour the batter in a greased slow cooker.
- Get another mixing bowl: Whisk in it the chocolate syrup, sugar and 1/4 C. warm water. Pour the mix all over the cake batter.
- Put on the lid and let them cook for 3 h on low. Serve your cake warm with some ice cream.
- Enjoy.

Servings Per Recipe: 8

Timing Information:

Preparation	15 mins
Total Time	3 hrs 15 mins

Nutritional Information:

Calories	388.0
Fat	17.1g
Cholesterol	53.0mg
Sodium	577.2mg
Carbohydrates	57.3g
Protein	5.7g

* Percent Daily Values are based on a 2,000 calorie diet.

SMOKED POTATO AND SAUSAGE GRATIN

Ingredients

- 2 -3 large potatoes, peeled and cut into bite sized pieces
- 1 (1 lb) package smoked sausage, cut into bite sized pieces
- 2 (14 1/2 oz) cans green beans, drained
- 1 small onion, quartered
- 1 garlic clove, minced
- 2 (10 1/2 oz) cans cream of mushroom soup, undiluted
- 1 C. shredded cheddar cheese

Directions

- Place the potato in the bottom of a greased slow cooker. Top it with the sausage followed by the green beans, onion, garlic, mushroom soup and cheddar cheese.
- Put on the lid let them cook for 4 h on low. Serve your gratin warm.
- Enjoy.

Servings Per Recipe: 6

Timing Information:

Preparation	10 mins
Total Time	6 hrs 10 mins

Nutritional Information:

Calories	535.6
Fat	33.9g
Cholesterol	66.0mg
Sodium	1456.8mg
Carbohydrates	39.3g
Protein	20.5g

* Percent Daily Values are based on a 2,000 calorie diet.

Velveeta Casserole

Ingredients

- 1 lb sausage
- 1 lb ground beef
- 1 lb Velveeta cheese
- 1 package rye bread

Directions

- Before you do anything, preheat the oven to 350 F.
- Place a large skillet over medium heat. Cook in it the sausage with beef for 12 min.
- Stir into it the cheese until it completely melts. Pour the mix in a greased casserole dish. Lay over it the rye bread.
- Place the casserole in the oven and cook it for 32 min then serve it hot.
- Enjoy.

Servings Per Recipe: 30

Timing Information:

Preparation	15 mins
Total Time	35 mins

Nutritional Information:

Calories	126.1
Fat	9.9g
Cholesterol	31.0mg
Sodium	371.5mg
Carbohydrates	1.8g
Protein	7.0g

* Percent Daily Values are based on a 2,000 calorie diet.

4-INGREDIENT POT ROAST

Ingredients

- 1 chuck roast
- garlic salt (to taste)
- pepper (to taste)
- 1 jar salsa

Directions

- Sprinkle some garlic salt and pepper all over the roast.
- Place in it in a greased slow cooker and pour the salsa all over it. Put on the lid and let it cook for 9 h.
- Once the time is up, drain the roast and shred it then stir it back into the pot or cook it in the oven to make it crispy for about 18 min then serve it hot.
- Enjoy.

Servings Per Recipe: 6

Timing Information:

Preparation	10 mins
Total Time	8 hrs 10 mins

Nutritional Information:

Calories	21.5
Fat	0.1g
Cholesterol	0.0mg
Sodium	479.1mg
Carbohydrates	5.0g
Protein	1.2g

* Percent Daily Values are based on a 2,000 calorie diet.

SPICY GARBANZO AND TURKEY STEW

Ingredients

- 1 1/2 lbs turkey tenderloins, cut into 3/4 inch pieces
- 1 tbsp chili powder
- 1 tsp ground cumin
- 3/4 tsp salt
- 1 (15 oz) cans diced tomatoes with mild green chilies
- 1 (15 oz) cans garbanzo beans, drained and rinsed (optional)
- 1 (15 oz) cans black beans, drained but not rinsed
- 1 (15 1/2 oz) cans pinto beans in chili sauce, un-drained
- 1 (4 oz) cans mild green chilies (optional)
- 1 red bell pepper, cut into 3/4 inch pieces
- 1 green bell pepper, cut into 3/4 inch pieces
- 3/4 C. onion, chopped
- 3/4 C. salsa
- 3 garlic cloves, minced
- fresh cilantro (optional)

Directions

- Combine the turkey tenderloins with chili powder, cumin and salt in a greased slow cooker.
- Stir into them the beans, tomatoes, chilies, bell peppers, onion, salsa and garlic.
- Put on the lid and let them cook for 6 h on low.
- Once the time is up, serve your stew hot.
- Enjoy.

Servings Per Recipe: 6

Timing Information:

| Preparation | 15 mins |
| Total Time | 5 hrs 15 mins |

Nutritional Information:

Calories	238.3
Fat	1.5g
Cholesterol	70.3mg
Sodium	850.1mg
Carbohydrates	22.0g
Protein	34.3g

* Percent Daily Values are based on a 2,000 calorie diet.

PASEO TILAPIA WITH SALSA

Ingredients

- 2 lbs tilapia fillets
- 1 1/2 C. tomatoes, chopped
- 1/2 C. green pepper, chopped
- 1/3 C. lemon juice
- 1 tbsp olive oil
- 2 tsp salt
- 2 tsp onions, minced
- 1 tsp basil leaves
- 1/4 C. black pepper, coarsely ground
- 4 drops red pepper sauce
- green pepper ring

Directions

- Before you do anything, preheat the oven to 500 F.
- Lay the fish fillets over a lined up cookie sheet.
- Get a large mixing bowl: Combine in it the tomato with green pepper, lemon juice, olive oil, onion, basil, pepper sauce, a pinch of salt and pepper to make the salsa.
- Spread the salsa over the fish fillets and cook them in the oven for 7 to 9 min.
- Serve your baked tilapia fillets with hot with some pepper rings.
- Enjoy.

Servings Per Recipe: 4

Timing Information:

Preparation	15 mins
Total Time	23 mins

Nutritional Information:

Calories	285.5
Fat	7.6g
Cholesterol	113.5mg
Sodium	1289.5mg
Carbohydrates	9.5g
Protein	47.1g

* Percent Daily Values are based on a 2,000 calorie diet.

Chicken Bop Dip

Ingredients

- 8 oz cream cheese
- 8 oz sour cream
- 1 (10 oz) cans white chicken meat, drained
- 1/2 tsp seasoning salt
- 1/4 medium onion, minced
- 1/4 C. parmesan cheese

Directions

- Before you do anything, preheat the oven to 375 F.
- Grease a casserole pan with some butter. Combine in it the cream cheese with sour cream, chicken, onion and a pinch of salt.
- Sprinkle the parmesan cheese on top. Place it in the oven and cook it for 32 min. Serve your dip hot with chips, veggies, bread...
- Enjoy.

Servings Per Recipe: 24

Timing Information:

| Preparation | 20 mins |
| Total Time | 50 mins |

Nutritional Information:

Calories	72.7
Fat	5.8g
Cholesterol	22.5mg
Sodium	57.2mg
Carbohydrates	0.8g
Protein	4.1g

* Percent Daily Values are based on a 2,000 calorie diet.

QUICK POT CAKE

Ingredients

- 1 (18 1/4 oz) boxes cake mix
- 1 can (12 oz.) soda pop

Directions

- Grease a slow cooker with a cooking spray.
- Whisk in it the cake mix with soda until no lumps are found. Put on the lid and cook the cake for 3 h on low.
- Serve your cake with some ice cream.
- Enjoy.

Servings Per Recipe: 1

Timing Information:

Preparation	5 mins
Total Time	3 hrs 5 mins

Nutritional Information:

Calories	2221.3
Fat	56.8g
Cholesterol	0.0mg
Sodium	3462.3mg
Carbohydrates	406.7g
Protein	23.4g

* Percent Daily Values are based on a 2,000 calorie diet.

CHICAGO ROAST DUMP DINNER

Ingredients

- 3 -5 lbs roast
- 2 cans cream of mushroom soup
- 2 cans beef broth
- 2 packets mushroom soup mix
- 1 beef bouillon cube
- 3 cans mushroom pieces, w/juice
- 1 medium onion, cut into pieces

Directions

- Whisk the mushroom soup with soup packets and broth in a slow cooker.
- Add in the roast with bouillon cube, mushroom, onion, a pinch of salt and pepper.
- Put on the lid and let them cook for 6 h on high. Serve your roast warm.
- Enjoy.

Servings Per Recipe: 6

Timing Information:

Preparation	10 mins
Total Time	6 hrs 10 mins

Nutritional Information:

Calories	800.5
Fat	56.9g
Cholesterol	158.0mg
Sodium	2810.5mg
Carbohydrates	21.4g
Protein	48.7g

* Percent Daily Values are based on a 2,000 calorie diet.

PEARLS STIR FRY

Ingredients

- 1 pint cherry tomatoes, halved
- 1 pint white pearl onion, trimmed
- 1/4 C. chicken broth
- 1/2 tsp superfine ground mustard
- 1/2-1 tsp dried parsley
- 1/4 tsp dried cumin
- salt

Directions

- Place a large pan over medium heat. Heat in it a splash of broth.
- Sauté in it the onion for 6 min. Add the tomato then lower the heat and let it cook for 5 while adding more broth if the mix is too dry.
- Stir in the parsley with mustard, cumin, and a pinch of salt then cook them for another minute.
- Enjoy.

Servings Per Recipe: 4

Timing Information:

Preparation	7 mins
Total Time	17 mins

Nutritional Information:

Calories	51.6
Fat	0.4g
Cholesterol	0.0mg
Sodium	54.1mg
Carbohydrates	11.2g
Protein	1.8g

* Percent Daily Values are based on a 2,000 calorie diet.

GOLDEN CHICKEN BREASTS WITH SHALLOT SALSA

Ingredients

- 1 1/2 lbs sweet potatoes, peeled and cut into 2-inch pieces
- 1 tbsp kosher salt, more to taste
- 1/2 tsp black pepper, more to taste
- 4 tbsp olive oil
- 24 oz chicken breasts, boneless and skinless
- 4 shallots, sliced into thin rings
- 2 tbsp rosemary, roughly chopped

Directions

- Bring a large pot of water to a boil. Cook in it the sweet potato with 1 tsp of salt for 18 min until it becomes tender.
- Drain the potato and place it aside. Reserve 1/4 C. of the cooking liquid. Place a large pan over medium heat. Melt 1 tbsp of butter in it. Sprinkle some salt and pepper over the chicken breasts.
- Place them in the hot pan and let them cook for 8 to 9 min on each side. Drain the chicken breasts and place them aside. Heat 3 tbsp of oil in the same skillet. Sauté in it the shallots, rosemary, 1/2 tsp salt, and 1/4 tsp pepper for 4 min to make the salsa.
- Serve your chicken breasts with the sweet potatoes and shallots salsa. Enjoy.

Servings Per Recipe: 4

Timing Information:

Preparation	10 mins
Total Time	30 mins

Nutritional Information:

Calories	574.5
Fat	29.4g
Cholesterol	108.8mg
Sodium	1947.9mg
Carbohydrates	37.9g
Protein	38.7g

* Percent Daily Values are based on a 2,000 calorie diet.

PERFECT PASTA SALAD

Ingredients

- 6 slices turkey bacon
- 1 1/4 C. Miracle Whip
- 2 tbsp sugar
- 1/2 tsp garlic salt
- 1 (16 oz) packages pasta, cooked and drained
- 3 carrots, shredded
- 1 green pepper, chopped
- 1 onion, chopped

Directions

- Place a large pan over medium heat. Cook in it the bacon until it become crisp. Drain it and place it aside.
- Get a large mixing bowl: Combine in it 2 tbsp of the bacon fat with the dressing, sugar and garlic salt.
- Stir in the miracle whip with pasta, carrot, pepper and onion. Toss them to coat.
- Place the pasta in the fridge for 32 min. Garnish it with bacon then serve it.
- Enjoy.

Servings Per Recipe: 12

Timing Information:

Preparation	30 mins
Total Time	1 hr

Nutritional Information:

Calories	213.1
Fat	5.7g
Cholesterol	7.7mg
Sodium	107.4mg
Carbohydrates	33.4g
Protein	6.5g

* Percent Daily Values are based on a 2,000 calorie diet.

LATIN VEGGIES CASSEROLE

Ingredients

- 2 (11 1/2 oz) cans corn mixed with chopped peppers, drained
- 1 (14 1/2 oz) cans tomatoes and green chilies, undrained
- 1 (15 1/2 oz) cans hominy, drained
- 1 (15 oz) cans black beans, drained and rinsed
- 1 (4 oz) cans chopped jalapenos, drained
- 2 tbsp fresh cilantro, chopped
- 1/2 tsp salt
- 1/4 tsp pepper
- 2/3 C. shredded low-fat Mexican cheese blend

Directions

- Before you do anything, preheat the oven to 350 F.
- Get a casserole dish and grease it with some butter. Toss in it all the ingredients except of the cheese.
- Place the casserole in the oven and let it cook for 26 min then serve it hot.
- Sprinkle the cheese over the veggies mix. Place the casserole back in the oven and let it cook for an extra 8 min then serve it hot.
- Enjoy.

Servings Per Recipe: 6

Timing Information:

Preparation	5 mins
Total Time	40 mins

Nutritional Information:

Calories	218.0
Fat	1.7g
Cholesterol	0.0mg
Sodium	1000.2mg
Carbohydrates	45.9g
Protein	8.9g

* Percent Daily Values are based on a 2,000 calorie diet.

ROTINI TURKEY STEW

Ingredients

- 3 tbsp extra virgin olive oil
- 1 green bell pepper, chopped
- 1 small yellow onion, chopped
- 3 large garlic cloves, minced
- 1 1/2 tsp Mexican seasoning
- 2 tbsp onion flakes
- 3/4 lb ground turkey thigh meat
- 28 oz medium salsa
- 1/2 C. water
- 1 tsp chili powder
- 1 tsp dried oregano
- 1 tsp sugar
- 1/2 tsp pepper
- 8 oz rotini pasta, uncooked
- 1 C. cheddar cheese, shredded

Directions

- Place a large pot over medium heat. Heat the olive oil in it.
- Cook in it the bell pepper for 3 min. Stir in the onion with garlic and cook them for 4 min.
- Stir in the seasoning mix with onion flakes and cook them for an extra 2 min.
- Mix in the turkey meat then cook them for 6 min.

- Place a large saucepan over medium heat. Stir in it the salsa with water, chili powder, dried oregano, sugar and pepper. Bring them to a boil.
- Stir the mix into the pot with the turkey and veggies. Stir in the pasta then cook them until they start boiling.
- Lower the heat and put on the lid. Cook the stew for 16 to 20 min over low heat. Once the time is up, serve it hot.
- Enjoy.

Servings Per Recipe: 4

Timing Information:

Preparation	15 mins
Total Time	35 mins

Nutritional Information:

Calories	607.7
Fat	24.6g
Cholesterol	88.3mg
Sodium	1449.9mg
Carbohydrates	63.0g
Protein	35.5g

* Percent Daily Values are based on a 2,000 calorie diet.

CHICAGO BREAKFAST PITAS

Ingredients

- 3 eggs
- 1 C. broccoli
- 2 slices muenster cheese
- salt and pepper
- 2 tbsp olive oil
- 1 pita bread, with no pocket

Directions

- Place a large skillet over medium heat. Heat the olive oil in it. Sauté in it the broccoli for 6 min.
- Stir in the eggs with a pinch of salt and pepper and scramble them in the pan. Cook them until the eggs are done.
- Lay the cheese slices on top and put on the lid. Turn off the heat and let the cheese melt.
- Transfer the eggs and broccoli mix to a serving plate.
- Heat a drizzle of olive oil in the same pan. Cook in it the pitta bread until it become golden on both sides for about 2 to 4 min.
- Serve it with the broccoli and eggs scramble.
- Enjoy.

Servings Per Recipe: 1

Timing Information:

Preparation	5 mins
Total Time	15 mins

Nutritional Information:

Calories	855.2
Fat	59.1g
Cholesterol	611.7mg
Sodium	916.8mg
Carbohydrates	41.1g
Protein	39.9g

* Percent Daily Values are based on a 2,000 calorie diet.

Teriyaki Wontons

Ingredients

- 1 -1 1/2 lb ground turkey
- 8 oz teriyaki sauce
- 4 oz water chestnuts, drained and diced
- 1 piece gingerroot, peeled and minced
- 8 oz hoisin sauce
- 12 oz wonton wrappers

Directions

- Get a large mixing bowl: Combine in it the turkey with the teriyaki sauce.
- Add to them the chestnuts with gingerroot, a pinch of salt and pepper. Mix them well to make the filling.
- Divide the filling on the wonton wrappers and wrap them, using water to seal the edges.
- Place a large skillet over medium heat. Grease it with a cooking spray or some oil. Cook in it the wrappers for 4 to 5 min on each side.
- Serve your stuffed wrappers with hoisin sauce.
- Enjoy.

Servings Per Recipe: 6

Timing Information:

Preparation	20 mins
Total Time	52 mins

Nutritional Information:

Calories	411.8
Fat	8.4g
Cholesterol	66.0mg
Sodium	2473.5mg
Carbohydrates	60.2g
Protein	22.5g

* Percent Daily Values are based on a 2,000 calorie diet.

CONDENSED MACARONI BAKE

Ingredients

- 2 C. uncooked elbow macaroni
- 3 C. cubed cooked chicken
- 1/2 C. cubed process American cheese
- 1 small onion, chopped
- 1/2 C. chopped celery
- 1/2 C. chopped green bell pepper
- 1 (8 oz) cans sliced water chestnuts, drained
- 1 (10 3/4 oz) cans condensed cream of mushroom soup, undiluted
- 1 (10 3/4 oz) cans condensed cream of chicken soup, undiluted
- 1 1/3 C. milk
- 1 (10 1/2 oz) cans chicken broth
- 1/4 C. butter, melted
- 2/3 C. crushed saltine
- 3/4 C. cashew halves

Directions

- Before you do anything, preheat the oven to 350 F. Grease a casserole dish with some butter.
- Lay in it the macaroni followed by the chicken on top, American cheese, onion, celery, bell pepper and chestnuts.
- Get a large mixing bowl: Whisk in it the mushroom soup, chicken soup, milk, a pinch of salt and pepper.
- Drizzle the mix all over the chestnut layer.

- Get a mixing bowl: Mix in it the butter with crushed saltine. Sprinkle the mix on top. Place the casserole in the oven and cook it for 38 to 42 min.
- Serve your macaroni casserole hot with some cashews on top.
- Enjoy.

Servings Per Recipe: 6

Timing Information:

Preparation	20 mins
Total Time	1 hr

Nutritional Information:

Calories	667.2
Fat	34.4g
Cholesterol	96.6mg
Sodium	1533.9mg
Carbohydrates	55.2g
Protein	34.7g

* Percent Daily Values are based on a 2,000 calorie diet.

CHICKEN RICE WITH CHEDDAR SAUCE

Ingredients

- 2 (10 3/4 oz) cans condensed cheddar cheese soup
- 1 C. water
- 2 C. salsa
- 1 1/4 C. uncooked white rice
- 2 lbs boneless skinless chicken, cubed
- 10 flour tortillas

Directions

- Grease a slow cooker with a cooking spray. Stir in it the soup, water, salsa, rice and chicken.
- Put on the lid and let them cook for 8 h on low.
- Serve your saucy chicken rice with some tortillas.
- Enjoy.

Servings Per Recipe: 10

Timing Information:

Preparation	15 mins
Total Time	8 hrs 15 mins

Nutritional Information:

Calories	367.0
Fat	8.6g
Cholesterol	66.8mg
Sodium	1018.3mg
Carbohydrates	42.5g
Protein	28.4g

* Percent Daily Values are based on a 2,000 calorie diet.

CHICAGO BLACK BEAN AND CREAM WRAPS

Ingredients

- 3 tbsp extra virgin olive oil
- 2 C. broccoli florets, sliced
- 1 red bell pepper, sliced
- 1 green bell pepper, sliced
- 1 small yellow onion, chopped
- 2 large garlic cloves, minced
- 1 tbsp chili powder
- 1/2 tsp garlic powder
- 1 (15 oz) cans black beans, rinsed and drained
- 1/2 C. low-fat sour cream
- 1/2 C. cheddar cheese, shredded
- 2 large flour tortillas

Directions

- Place a large pan over medium heat. Heat the olive oil in it. Sauté in it the bell pepper with broccoli for 4 min.
- Stir in the garlic with onion and cook them for 5 min. Stir in the chili powder and garlic powder. Cook them for 1 min.
- Stir in the black beans and heat it through. Turn off the heat. Fold the sour cream with cheddar cheese into the hot mix.

- Spoon it into tortillas and wrap them then serve them right away with your favorite toppings.
- Enjoy.

Servings Per Recipe: 2

Timing Information:

Preparation	15 mins
Total Time	30 mins

Nutritional Information:

Calories	1016.3
Fat	47.6g
Cholesterol	53.2mg
Sodium	1018.6mg
Carbohydrates	114.9g
Protein	36.3g

* Percent Daily Values are based on a 2,000 calorie diet.

HOMEMADE BLUEBERRY BLINTZES

Ingredients

- 1 lb cream-style cottage cheese
- 1 lb farmer cheese, shredded
- 2 eggs
- 1/4 tsp salt
- 1/4-1/2 C. granulated sugar
- 1/2 tsp vanilla extract
- 1 lemon, juice of
- 1 C. butter, melted and cooled slightly
- 2 eggs
- 1/4 C. milk
- 3 tsp baking powder
- 1/2 C. sugar
- 1 C. flour
- 1 tsp vanilla extract
- sugar
- cinnamon
- 1 (21 oz) cans blueberry pie filling
- 1/2 tsp grated lemon, rind of

Directions

- Before you do anything, preheat the oven to 300 F.
- Get a large mixing bowl: Beat in it the cottage cheese with farmer cheese, eggs, sugar, vanilla and salt until they become smooth.
- Get another mixing bowl: Whisk in it the lemon juice with butter, 2 eggs, milk, baking powder, vanilla, sugar, and flour until no lumps are found.
- Spread half of the mix in a baking dish. Top it with all of the cheese mix. Spread the remaining flour batter on top.

- Get a small mixing bowl: Mix in it some sugar with cinnamon. Lay all over the cake pan.
- Place the baking pan in the oven and cook it for 50 to 60 min.
- Garnish your cake with the blueberry pie filling and grated lemon after it cools down then serve it.
- Enjoy.

Servings Per Recipe: 1

Timing Information:

Preparation	30 mins
Total Time	1 hr 30 mins

Nutritional Information:

Calories	4963.0
Fat	231.0g
Cholesterol	1442.3mg
Sodium	5260.5mg
Carbohydrates	542.9g
Protein	179.4g

* Percent Daily Values are based on a 2,000 calorie diet.

Classic Chicken and Broccoli Casserole

Ingredients

- 2 (10 oz) packages frozen broccoli, steamed
- 2 C. cooked chicken
- 2 cans cream of chicken soup
- 1 C. mayonnaise
- 1 tsp lemon juice
- 1/2 C. shredded cheese
- 1 tbsp butter
- breadcrumbs

Directions

- Before you do anything, preheat the oven to 300 F. Coat a casserole dish with some butter.
- Place the broccoli in the casserole dish then top it with the chicken.
- Get a mixing bowl: Whisk in it the mayonnaise with chicken soup, lemon juice, a pinch of salt and pepper. Pour the mix all over the broccoli and chicken mix.
- Get a mixing bowl: Mix in some breadcrumbs with butter. Spread it all over them then top it with the shredded cheese.
- Place the casserole in the oven for 48 min. Serve it hot.
- Enjoy.

Servings Per Recipe: 4

Timing Information:

Preparation	20 mins
Total Time	1 hr 5 mins

Nutritional Information:

Calories	591.1
Fat	39.8g
Cholesterol	96.6mg
Sodium	1660.0mg
Carbohydrates	33.0g
Protein	28.4g

* Percent Daily Values are based on a 2,000 calorie diet.

Bell Beef and Rice Soup

Ingredients

- 1 lb ground beef
- 1/2 chopped onion
- 3 bell peppers, any type
- 14 oz diced tomatoes
- 1 (8 oz) cans tomato sauce
- 1 1/2 C. water
- 1/4 C. balsamic vinegar
- 1/8 tsp salt
- 1/8 tsp black pepper
- 1/4 C. brown sugar
- 1 C. V8 vegetable juice
- 1/2 C. Minute Rice

Directions

- Place a large skillet over medium heat. Cook in it the beef with onion, garlic, pepper, a pinch of salt and pepper for 12 min.
- Combine the tomato sauce with water, vinegar, sugar, veggies juice, a pinch of salt and pepper in a large saucepan.
- Cook them until they start boiling. Stir in the rice and let them cook for 6 min with the lid on.
- Once the time is up, drain the beef mixture and stir it into the soup pot. Put on the lid and cook it for 16 min over low heat. Serve it hot.
- Enjoy.

Servings Per Recipe: 6

Timing Information:

Preparation	15 mins
Total Time	35 mins

Nutritional Information:

Calories	281.2
Fat	11.7g
Cholesterol	51.4mg
Sodium	390.8mg
Carbohydrates	27.4g
Protein	16.6g

* Percent Daily Values are based on a 2,000 calorie diet.

CHUNKY AND CHEESY TACO DIP

Ingredients

- 5 oz Swanson white chicken meat packed in water, drained
- 10 oz mild chunky salsa
- 1 1/4 oz taco seasoning
- 2 C. shredded cheddar cheese

Directions

- Place a heavy saucepan over medium heat. Stir all the ingredients in it and heat everything through for 3 min.
- Serve your dip with some chips, bread, veggies.
- Enjoy.

Servings Per Recipe: 6

Timing Information:

Preparation	15 mins
Total Time	17 mins

Nutritional Information:

Calories	208.0
Fat	14.4g
Cholesterol	51.3mg
Sodium	549.3mg
Carbohydrates	3.6g
Protein	16.0g

* Percent Daily Values are based on a 2,000 calorie diet.

RED POTATOES AND ROOT VEGETABLES

Ingredients

- 8 C. chopped red potatoes
- 4 C. chopped parsnips
- 1 rutabaga, peeled and chopped
- 1 onion, chopped
- 2 tsp salt, divided
- 1 (8 oz) packages cream cheese, softened
- 1/2 C. butter

Directions

- Bring a large pot of water to a boil with 1 tsp of salt.
- Stir in it the rutabaga with potato, and parsnips. Put on the lid and let them cook for 14 min over medium heat.
- Once the time is up, discard the water and transfer the cooked veggies to a large mixing bowl.
- Add to it the cream cheese with butter and mix them well. Adjust the seasoning of the salad then serve it.
- Enjoy.

Servings Per Recipe: 10

Timing Information:

Preparation	10 mins
Total Time	22 mins

Nutritional Information:

Calories	301.2
Fat	17.4g
Cholesterol	49.3mg
Sodium	654.1mg
Carbohydrates	33.7g
Protein	4.9g

* Percent Daily Values are based on a 2,000 calorie diet.

How to Make a Hot Dog Chicago Style

Ingredients

- 1 all-beef hot dog
- 1 poppy seed hot dog bun
- 1 tbsp yellow mustard
- 1 tbsp sweet green pickle relish
- 1 tbsp chopped onion
- 4 tomato wedges
- 1 dill pickle spear
- 2 sport peppers
- 1 dash celery salt

Directions

- Place a large saucepan of water over medium heat and bring it to a boil. Place a steamer on top and lay the hot dog in it. Let it cook for 3 min.
- Lay the hot dog in the bun then top it with the yellow mustard, sweet green pickle relish, onion, tomato wedges, pickle spear, sport peppers, and celery salt.
- Serve your hot dog right away.
- Enjoy.

Servings Per Recipe: 1

Timing Information:

Preparation	10 m
Cooking	5 m
Total Time	15 m

Nutritional Information:

Calories	377 kcal
Fat	19.7 g
Carbohydrates	38g
Protein	12.4 g
Cholesterol	30 mg
Sodium	2387 mg

* Percent Daily Values are based on a 2,000 calorie diet.

DEMPSTER DIP

Ingredients

- 1 (10 ounce) package frozen chopped spinach, thawed and drained
- 1 C. sour cream
- 1 C. mayonnaise
- 3/4 C. chopped green onions
- 2 tsps dried parsley
- 1 tsp lemon juice
- 1/2 tsp seasoned salt
- 1 (1 lb) loaf round, crusty Italian bread

Directions

- Get a mixing bowl: Whisk in it the spinach, sour cream, mayonnaise, green onions, parsley, lemon juice, and salt.
- Place the dip in the fridge until ready to serve. Serve it with some bread or veggies.
- Enjoy.

Servings Per Recipe: 10

Timing Information:

Preparation	
Cooking	15 m
Total Time	20 m

Nutritional Information:

Calories	341 kcal
Fat	24.1 g
Carbohydrates	26.3g
Protein	6.1 g
Cholesterol	18 mg
Sodium	471 mg

* Percent Daily Values are based on a 2,000 calorie diet.

PIZZA SKILLET

Ingredients

- 1 (1 lb) loaf frozen bread dough, thawed
- 1 lb bulk Italian sausage, crumbled
- 2 C. shredded mozzarella cheese
- 8 ounces sliced fresh mushrooms
- 1 small onion, chopped
- 2 tsps olive oil
- 1 (28 ounce) can diced tomatoes, drained
- 3/4 tsp dried oregano
- 1/2 tsp salt
- 1/4 tsp fennel seed
- 1/4 tsp garlic powder
- 1/2 C. freshly grated Parmesan cheese

Directions

- Before you do anything, preheat the oven to 350 F. Spread the dough in the bottom of a greased oven proof skillet.
- Place a large pan over medium heat. Cook in it the sausages for 6 min. Drain it and spread it over the dough followed by the mozzarella cheese.
- Heat the olive oil in the same pan where the sausages were cooked. Sauté in the onion with mushroom for 4 min.
- Add the tomatoes, oregano, salt, fennel seed and garlic powder. Cook them for 1 min. Spread the mix all over the pizza top it with the parmesan cheese.
- Cook the pizza skillet in the oven for 30 to 35 min. Serve it hot. Enjoy.

Servings Per Recipe: 6

Timing Information:

Preparation	30 m
Cooking	35 m
Total Time	1 h 5 m

Nutritional Information:

Calories	578 kcal
Fat	27.4 g
Carbohydrates	46.8g
Protein	32.3 g
Cholesterol	61 mg
Sodium	1816 mg

* Percent Daily Values are based on a 2,000 calorie diet.

DEEP DISH DOUGH

Ingredients

- 2 1/4 tsps active dry yeast
- 1 1/2 tsps white sugar
- 1 1/8 C. warm water
- 3 C. all-purpose flour
- 1/2 C. corn oil
- 1 1/2 tsps kosher salt

Directions

- Get a small mixing bowl: Stir in it the yeast with sugar and warm water let it sit for few minutes to dissolve.
- Get a large mixing bowl: Mix in it the yeast mixture, flour, corn oil, and kosher salt with your hands or a stand mixer until you get a soft dough.
- Shape it into a ball and place it in a greased bowl. Lay a kitchen towel over it and let it rise for 6 h.
- Once the time is up, remove it from the bowl and let it rest for 14 min. Roll the dough into a 10 inch circle then add to it your favorite toppings and cook it!
- Enjoy.

Servings Per Recipe: 8

Timing Information:

Preparation	
Cooking	10 m
Total Time	6 h 25 m

Nutritional Information:

Calories	299 kcal
Fat	14.3 g
Carbohydrates	37g
Protein	5.3 g
Cholesterol	0 mg
Sodium	362 mg

* Percent Daily Values are based on a 2,000 calorie diet.

SIX CORNERS PIZZA

Ingredients

- 2 tsps white sugar
- 1 C. warm water (110 degrees F/45 degrees C)
- 1 tsp active dry yeast
- 3 C. unbleached all-purpose flour, divided
- 1/2 C. warm water (110 degrees F/45 degrees C)
- 1/2 C. yellow cornmeal
- 1 1/2 tsps salt
- 2 tbsps olive oil
- 1/4 lb spicy Italian sausage
- 9 ounces shredded mozzarella cheese
- 1/4 C. grated Parmesan cheese
- 1/3 C. diced pepperoni
- 1/4 C. chopped onion
- 1/8 C. chopped green bell pepper
- 1 tsp dried oregano
- 3 cloves garlic, sliced
- 1/2 C. tomato sauce

Directions

- To prepare the dough:
- Get a small mixing bowl: Stir in it the sugar with 1 C. f warm water then let it sit to dissolve.
- Get a large mixing bowl: Mix in it the yeast, 1/2 C. flour, and 1/2 C. warm water. Let them sit for 22 min.
- Get a mixing bowl: Stir in it the rest of the 2 1/2 C. flour with cornmeal and salt. Reserve half of the mix dry aside.

- Add the sugar and water mix into the mixture in the bowl and mix them well. Add to it the reserved flour mix and stir them well.
- Add the flour and yeast mix then combine them well until you get a soft dough. Place the dough on a floured working surface and knead it with your hands for 10 min.
- Transfer it to an oil greased large bowl and lay a piece of plastic wrap over it. Place it aside until it rises and double.
- Before you do anything, preheat the oven to 450 F.
- Get a large mixing bowl: Mix in it the sausage, mozzarella cheese, Parmesan cheese, pepperoni, onion, bell pepper, oregano and garlic to make the filling.
- Divide the pizza dough into 2 pieces. Press 1 piece of dough into the bottom of a greased baking pan.
- Place it in the oven and cook it for 5 min. spread over it the filling. Roll the remaining dough pieces and drape it over the filling.
- Press the edges with a fork. Use a sharp knife to make 2 slits in the top dough piece and pour the tomato sauce all over it.
- Place the pan in the lower rack and cook it for 46 min. serve your pizza warm.
- Enjoy.

Servings Per Recipe: 5

Timing Information:

Preparation	1 h
Cooking	50 m
Total Time	1 h 50 m

Nutritional Information:

Calories	703 kcal
Fat	30 g
Carbohydrates	75.8g
Protein	30.5 g
Cholesterol	70 mg
Sodium	1646 mg

* Percent Daily Values are based on a 2,000 calorie diet.

CHICAGO CITY CHILI

Ingredients

- 2 lbs ground beef
- 4 (14.5 ounce) cans kidney beans
- 4 (15 ounce) cans diced tomatoes
- 1 (12 ounce) bottle tomato-based chili sauce
- 1 large white onion, chopped
- 6 cloves garlic, minced
- 2 tbsps chili seasoning
- 1 tsp black pepper
- 1/2 tsp garlic powder
- 1/2 tsp onion powder
- 1/2 tsp cayenne pepper
- 1/2 tsp oregano
- 1/4 C. sugar
- 1 tsp hot sauce
- 1 tsp Worcestershire sauce

Directions

- Place a Dutch oven over medium heat. Cook in it the beef for 8 min. discard the excess fat.
- Stir in the remaining ingredients. Cook them until they start boiling. Lower the heat and put on the lid.
- Cook the stew for 4 h while stirring every once in a while then serve it warm.
- Enjoy.

Servings Per Recipe: 10

Timing Information:

Preparation	15 m
Cooking	4 h
Total Time	4 h 15 m

Nutritional Information:

Calories	389 kcal
Fat	11.5 g
Carbohydrates	41.4g
Protein	26.3 g
Cholesterol	55 mg
Sodium	890 mg

* Percent Daily Values are based on a 2,000 calorie diet.

FULL MACARONI SALAD

Ingredients

- 1 (8 ounce) package salad macaroni
- 1 C. small broccoli florets
- 3/4 C. diced Cheddar cheese
- 1/2 C. chopped green bell pepper
- 1/2 C. dill pickle relish, with juice
- 1 large dill pickle, chopped
- 1/2 C. chopped celery
- 1/2 C. sliced black olives
- 1/2 C. sliced green olives (optional)
- 1/4 C. chopped green onion
- 2 tbsps shredded carrot
- 1 tbsp chopped pimento peppers
- 1 C. light mayonnaise
- 1/4 C. prepared yellow mustard
- 1 tsp salt
- 1/2 tsp white sugar
- 1/4 tsp black pepper

Directions

- Cook the pasta according to the directions on the package. Drain it.
- Get a large mixing bowl: Toss in it the macaroni, broccoli, Cheddar cheese, green pepper, pickle relish, dill pickle, celery, black olives, green olives, green onion, carrot, and pimento.

- Get a small mixing bowl: Whisk in it the mayonnaise, mustard, salt, sugar, and black pepper to make the sauce.
- Add the sauce to the salad and toss them to coat. Place it in the fridge for at least 4 h then serve it.
- Enjoy.

Servings Per Recipe: 10

Timing Information:

Preparation	30 m
Cooking	10 m
Total Time	4 h 40 m

Nutritional Information:

Calories	197 kcal
Fat	7.4 g
Carbohydrates	26.8g
Protein	6.4 g
Cholesterol	10 mg
Sodium	1143 mg

* Percent Daily Values are based on a 2,000 calorie diet.

ITALIAN BEEF LUNCH

Ingredients

- 1 1/2 lbs boneless beef chuck, cut into 2-inch pieces
- salt and ground black pepper to taste
- 1 tbsp vegetable oil
- 6 cloves garlic, sliced
- 2 tbsps white vinegar
- 1 tbsp dried oregano
- 1 1/2 tsps salt, or to taste
- 1 tsp dried thyme
- 1 tsp dried rosemary
- 1 tsp freshly ground black pepper
- 1 bay leaf
- 1/4 tsp red pepper flakes, or to taste
- 3 C. chicken broth, or as needed
- 4 ciabatta rolls, sliced in half
- 1 C. chopped giardiniera
- 2 tsps chopped fresh flat-leaf parsley

Directions

- Sprinkle some sat and pepper all over the chuck roast.
- Place a large pot over medium heat. Heat the vegetable oil in it and brown in it the meat for 3 to 5 min on each side.
- Add the garlic, vinegar, oregano, 1 1/2 tsps salt, thyme, rosemary, 1 tsp black pepper, bay leaf, and red pepper flakes.
- Stir in the broth and put on the lid. Cook them until they start simmering.

- Put on the lid and cook them for 1 h 25 min over low heat. Pour the mix in a colander to drain the meat. Reserve the broth in the pot.
- Cut the beef chuck into pieces and cover it with a piece of foil.
- Place the rolls on a pan. Place on it 1 half of the rolls and spread over them 2 tbsps of the reserved broth for each one.
- Lay on each roll half a large spoon of the pickled veggies and beef chuck. Cover them with the top buns and place them aside.
- Heat the beef broth and skim the fat then serve it hot with the sandwiches.
- Enjoy.

Servings Per Recipe: 4

Timing Information:

Preparation	15 m
Cooking	1 h 10 m
Total Time	1 h 25 m

Nutritional Information:

Calories	417 kcal
Fat	16.1 g
Carbohydrates	36.5g
Protein	30.1 g
Cholesterol	82 mg
Sodium	2119 mg

* Percent Daily Values are based on a 2,000 calorie diet.

CHICAGO RESTAURANT DUCK

Ingredients

- 1 (4 lb) whole duck
- 1 tbsp garlic powder
- 1 tbsp onion powder
- salt and pepper, to taste
- 2 tbsps caraway seeds

Directions

- Before you do anything, preheat the oven to 425 F.
- Rinse the duck and dry it with some paper towels. Use a sharp knife to score it several times.
- Sprinkle some garlic powder, onion powder, salt, and pepper inside and outside of the duck. Rub the caraway seeds all over it.
- Place the duck on a roasting pan with the breast facing down. Let it cook for 16 min. Flip the duck and cook it for an extra 16 min.
- Lower the oven temperature to 350 F. Cook in it the duck with the breast for an extra 22 min.
- Flip it to face the breast down and cook it for an extra 22 min. Once the time is up, wrap it in a piece of foil and let it rest for 12 min then serve it.
- Enjoy.

Servings Per Recipe: 4

Timing Information:

Preparation	15 m
Cooking	1 h 10 m
Total Time	1 h 35 m

Nutritional Information:

Calories	389 kcal
Fat	31.3 g
Carbohydrates	4.5g
Protein	21.8 g
Cholesterol	91 mg
Sodium	163 mg

* Percent Daily Values are based on a 2,000 calorie diet.

CHICAGO CUB'S ITALIAN DIP

Ingredients

- 1 (1.37 ounce) package McCormick Spaghetti Sauce Mix
- 1 C. part-skim ricotta cheese
- 1 egg
- 2 C. shredded mozzarella cheese, divided
- 1/2 C. grated Parmesan cheese
- 1/4 C. mini pepperoni slices

Directions

- Before you do anything, preheat the oven to 375 F.
- Make the sauce according to the directions on the package.
- Get a large mixing bowl: Combine in it the ricotta cheese, egg, 1 C. of the mozzarella cheese and Parmesan cheese.
- Pour the mix in a greased casserole dish. Spread over it 1 C. of mozzarella cheese and pepperoni.
- Place the pizza casserole in the oven and cook it for 22 min. Serve it with some bread.
- Enjoy.

Servings Per Recipe: 32

Timing Information:

Preparation	5 m
Cooking	20 m
Total Time	25 m

Nutritional Information:

Calories	49 kcal
Fat	3 g
Carbohydrates	1.5g
Protein	3.7 g
Cholesterol	16 mg
Sodium	165 mg

* Percent Daily Values are based on a 2,000 calorie diet.

BALLPARK SALMON

Ingredients

- cooking spray
- 4 (6 ounce) salmon fillets
- 1/4 lemon, juiced
- 2 tsps dried dill weed
- 1/4 C. Dijon mustard
- 2 large dill pickles, diced
- 1/2 white onion, diced
- 1 tomato, seeded and diced
- 4 sport peppers, chopped, or to taste (optional)
- 1 dash celery seed, or to taste

Directions

- Before you do anything, preheat the oven to 400 F.
- Get a 4 large pieces of foil and grease them with a cooking spray.
- Lay the salmon fillets in the foil pieces. Pour over them the lemon juice, dill weed, 1 tbsp mustard, dill pickle, onion, a pinch of salt and pepper.
- Wrap the foil pieces over the salmon fillets and place them on a cookie sheet. Cook them in oven for 16 min.
- Once the time is up, place the salmon packets on serving plates. Open them and top them with the diced tomatoes, celery seeds and sport peppers. Serve them hot.
- Enjoy.

Servings Per Recipe: 4

Timing Information:

Preparation	20 m
Cooking	15 m
Total Time	35 m

Nutritional Information:

Calories	312 kcal
Fat	16.5 g
Carbohydrates	8.8g
Protein	29.8 g
Cholesterol	83 mg
Sodium	1581 mg

* Percent Daily Values are based on a 2,000 calorie diet.

FULL ITALIAN BEEF

Ingredients

- 1 (5 lb) rump roast
- 1/2 tsp garlic powder
- 1/2 tsp dried oregano
- 1/2 tsp coarse-grind black pepper

Sauce

- 2 C. boiling water
- 2 beef bouillon cubes
- 2 tsps dried oregano
- 1 tsp dried thyme
- 1/2 tsp coarse-grind black pepper, to taste
- 1 tsp Tabasco sauce
- 8 garlic cloves, minced
- 2 tbsps Worcestershire sauce
- salt

Directions

- Before you do anything, preheat the oven to 325 F.
- Season the garlic powder, oregano, salt and pepper. Place the roast in a roasting pan and cook it in the oven for 2 h 35 min.
- Once the time is up, cover the roast with a piece of foil and let it rest for 10 min.
- Stir the boiling water, bouillon cubes, oregano, thyme, pepper, Tabasco sauce, garlic and Worcestershire sauce into the roasting pan with the remaining drippings from the roast.
- Place it over medium heat and cook it for 22 min while stirring from time to time to make the gravy.

- Slice the roast thinly and stir it into the hot gravy. Allow it to cool down for a while then place it in the fridge for at least 8 min.
- Heat your roast gravy then serve it warm with some steamed or roasted veggies.
- Enjoy.

Servings Per Recipe: 7

Timing Information:

Preparation	8 hrs 15 mins
Total Time	10 hrs 45 mins

Nutritional Information:

Calories	657.6
Fat	39.5g
Cholesterol	243.1mg
Sodium	517.7mg
Carbohydrates	3.2g
Protein	67.7g

* Percent Daily Values are based on a 2,000 calorie diet.

Maria's Italian Beef

Ingredients

- 5 lbs rump roast
- 2 (10 1/4 ounce) cans broth
- 1 (1 ounce) package Italian salad dressing mix
- pepperoncini pepper
- 1 jar giardiniera
- 3 -5 sweet green peppers
- 1 loaf long thin French bread

Directions

- Grease a crockpot with some butter. Stir in it the roast with your broth, Italian dressing mix, pepperoncini, giardiniera, a pinch of salt and pepper.
- Put on the lid and cook them for 6 h on low. Flip the roast and cook them another 6 h on low.
- Once the time is up, flip the roast again and let it cook for another 6 h on low.
- Slice the sweet peppers into 1/8 inch slices and blanch them in some hot water until they become tender. Drain them and place them aside.
- Slice the bread into 6 inches slices and pull them open. Drain the roast and shred it then spoon it into the bread pieces.
- Drizzle over it some of sauce from the pot if you desire then serve them hot.
- Enjoy.

Servings Per Recipe: 1

Timing Information:

Preparation	10 mins
Total Time	18 hrs 10 mins

Nutritional Information:

Calories	1519.3
Fat	58.9g
Cholesterol	340.2mg
Sodium	2052.1mg
Carbohydrates	119.8g
Protein	121.5g

* Percent Daily Values are based on a 2,000 calorie diet.

ITALIAN BEEF II

Ingredients

- 1 tsp salt
- 1 tsp black pepper, ground
- 1 tsp oregano
- 1 tsp basil
- 1 tsp onion salt
- 2 -3 C. water, or broth
- 1 tsp parsley
- 1 tsp garlic powder
- 1 bay leaf
- 1 (2/3 ounce) package dried Italian salad dressing mix
- 5 lbs rump roast
- 3 beef bouillon cubes (optional)
- 1 green pepper, sliced (optional)

Directions

- Place a large pot over medium heat. Stir in it the salt, pepper, oregano, basil, onion salt, water, parsley, garlic powder, water, bay leaf and salad dressing mix.
- Cook them until they start boiling to make the sauce.
- Grease a slow cooker with a cooking spray. Lay in it the roast and coat it with the sauce. Put on the lid and let it cook for 11 h on low.
- Once the time is up, discard the bay leaf. Drain the roast and shred it then stir it back into the pot. Stir in the bouillon cubes with pepper.
- Let it sit for 45 min. Spoon the creamy beef into bread rolls and serve them warm.
- Enjoy.

Servings Per Recipe: 10

Timing Information:

Preparation	30 mins
Total Time	6 hrs 30 mins

Nutritional Information:

Calories	451.6
Fat	27.5g
Cholesterol	170.1mg
Sodium	354.6mg
Carbohydrates	0.6g
Protein	47.0g

* Percent Daily Values are based on a 2,000 calorie diet.

SQUASH AND STEAKS IN THE PRESSURE COOKER

Ingredients

- 2 1/2 lbs round steaks, cut 1/2-inch thick
- 1 C. flour
- 1 tsp salt
- 1/2 tsp pepper
- 1 C. fresh breadcrumb
- 1 1/4 C. chopped onions
- 2 C. finely chopped butternut squash
- 1/4 C. chopped green pepper
- 1/4 C. chopped celery
- 1 tsp salt
- 1 egg, beaten
- 2 tbsps margarine, melted
- 1/4 C. margarine
- 1 C. water

Directions

- Slice the steaks into 8 pieces in total.
- Get a shallow dish: Mix in it the flour with 1 tsp salt, and pepper. Dust the steak pieces with the flour mix.
- Get a large mixing bowl: Mix in it the bread crumbs, onion, squash, green pepper, celery, 1 tsp salt, egg, and 2 tbsps melted margarine. to make the filling.
- Lay 1/8 of the filling over 1 steak piece and roll it around it tightly. Secure it with a toothpick. Repeat the process with the remaining ingredients.

- Press the sauté button on a pressure cooker and melt in it 1/4 C. margarine. Lay in it the steak rolls and cook them for 3 to 4 min on each side.
- Drain them and place them aside. Pour 1 C. of water in the pot and lower in it a steamer basket.
- Place the browned steak rolls in the basket. Put on the lid and cook them for 16 min. serve them warm with your favorite toppings.
- Enjoy.

Servings Per Recipe: 8

Timing Information:

Preparation	20 mins
Total Time	35 mins

Nutritional Information:

Calories	494.8
Fat	26.4g
Cholesterol	126.7mg
Sodium	874.4mg
Carbohydrates	28.6g
Protein	34.3g

* Percent Daily Values are based on a 2,000 calorie diet.

Italian Pizza Minis

Ingredients

- 1 refrigerated thin pizza crust, or homemade
- 3 1/2 ounces pepperoni
- 1/2 C. buttermilk ranch dressing
- 3 green onions, chopped
- 1/2 C. mozzarella cheese, shredded
- 1 C. Monterey Jack cheese, shredded

Directions

- Before you do anything, preheat the oven to 425 F.
- Lay the dough on a working surface. Pour the ranch dressing all over it. Top it with the pepperoni, green onions and cheese.
- Roll the dough over the filling and place it on a baking pan. Cook the pizza in the oven for 16 min then serve it warm.
- Enjoy.

Servings Per Recipe: 4

Timing Information:

Preparation	15 mins
Total Time	30 mins

Nutritional Information:

Calories	417.2
Fat	37.9g
Cholesterol	71.8mg
Sodium	974.1mg
Carbohydrates	3.3g
Protein	16.0g

* Percent Daily Values are based on a 2,000 calorie diet.

WEST TOWN SPICY RELISH

Ingredients

- 1/2 peck ripe tomatoes, diced
- 1 C. onion, minced
- 2 green bell peppers, chopped
- 1 hot red pepper, chopped
- 1 1/2 C. celery, chopped
- 1 C. sugar
- 4 tbsps salt
- 3 C. cider vinegar
- 1/2 C. mustard seeds
- 2 tbsps nutmeg
- 2 tsps ground cinnamon
- 1 tsp clove

Directions

- Drain the tomato from all the juices.
- Get a mixing bowl: Toss in it the tomato with onions, peppers and celery.
- Get a small mixing bowl: Whisk in it the sugar and salt, vinegar, mustard seed and spices.
- Add the mix to the veggies and toss them to coat. Pour it sterilized mason jars and place them in the fridge for a least 3 days before serving it.
- Enjoy.

Servings Per Recipe: 1

Timing Information:

Preparation	20 mins
Total Time	20 mins

Nutritional Information:

Calories	359.7
Fat	6.2g
Cholesterol	0.0mg
Sodium	7025.0mg
Carbohydrates	67.5g
Protein	5.1g

* Percent Daily Values are based on a 2,000 calorie diet.

DePaul Glazed Meatballs

Ingredients

Meatball

- 1 1/2 lbs hamburger
- 1/4 C. breadcrumbs
- 2 eggs
- 1 (1 1/4 ounce) packages onion soup mix

Glazed

- 1/2 C. brown sugar
- 1 (12 ounce) jars chili sauce
- 6 ounces water
- 1 (16 ounce) cans sauerkraut
- 1 (16 ounce) cans whole berry cranberry sauce

Directions

- Before you do anything, preheat the oven to 350 F.
- Get a large mixing bowl: Combine in it the meatballs ingredients. Shape them into bite size meatballs.
- Get a mixing bowl: Whisk in it the sauce ingredients.
- Place the meatballs in a greased casserole dish and pour the sauce all over them. Cook it in the oven for 1 h 35 min. Serve it hot.
- Enjoy.

Servings Per Recipe: 6

Timing Information:

Preparation	10 mins
Total Time	1 hr 40 mins

Nutritional Information:

Calories	535.0
Fat	15.5g
Cholesterol	146.9mg
Sodium	1923.7mg
Carbohydrates	69.0g
Protein	28.8g

* Percent Daily Values are based on a 2,000 calorie diet.

OATMEAL CHOCOLATE COOKIES

Ingredients

- 3 1/2 C. flour
- 3 tsps baking soda
- 1 tsp salt
- 1 C. butter
- 1 C. brown sugar
- 1 C. sugar
- 1 egg
- 1 tbsp milk
- 2 tsps vanilla
- 1 C. vegetable oil
- 1 1/2 C. Rice Krispies
- 1 1/2 C. oatmeal
- 12 ounces chocolate chips

Directions

- Before you do anything, preheat the oven to 350 F.
- Get a large mixing bowl: Stir in it the flour, baking soda, and salt.
- Get a mixing bowl: Mix in it the butter, sugars and egg, milk, and vanilla with an electric mixer until they become smooth.
- Add to it the flour mix with the vegetable oil gradually while alternating between them and mixing at the same time.
- Fold the cereal, oatmeal and chocolate chips into the mixture. Use a large spoon to place the mixture in the shape of mounds on a lined up baking sheet.
- Place the cookie in the oven and cook them for 9 to 11 min.
- Once the time is up, allow the cookies to cool down completely then serve them. Enjoy.

Servings Per Recipe: 24

Timing Information:

Preparation	35 mins
Total Time	45 mins

Nutritional Information:

Calories	379.9
Fat	21.7g
Cholesterol	28.1mg
Sodium	45.3g
Carbohydrates	3.6g
Protein	379.9

* Percent Daily Values are based on a 2,000 calorie diet.

SHRIMP CASSEROLE

Ingredients

- 2 lbs medium shrimp
- 1/2 C. butter, melted
- 1/4 C. dry sherry
- 2 garlic cloves, minced
- 2 tbsps finely chopped fresh parsley
- 1 tbsp finely chopped fresh chives
- ground nutmeg
- salt, to taste
- cayenne pepper, to taste
- 1 C. dry breadcrumbs

Directions

- Before you do anything, preheat the oven to 350 F.
- Bring a large pot of water to a boil. Place in it the shrimp and cook it until it starts boiling again.
- Drain the shrimp, peel it and devein it.
- Get a large mixing bowl: Whisk in it the butter, sherry, garlic, parsley, chives, nutmeg, salt, and cayenne pepper.
- Combine in the breadcrumbs. Spread half of the cooked shrimp in a greased casserole dish.
- Spread over it the breadcrumbs mix. Top it with the remaining shrimp and the breadcrumbs mix on top.
- Place the casserole in the oven and cook it for 32 min. Serve your shrimp casserole hot.
- Enjoy.

Servings Per Recipe: 6

Timing Information:

Preparation	1 hr
Total Time	1 hr 30 mins

Nutritional Information:

Calories	410.9
Fat	18.9g
Cholesterol	271.0mg
Sodium	16.1g
Carbohydrates	33.5g
Protein	410.9

* Percent Daily Values are based on a 2,000 calorie diet.

EGG SALAD CHICAGO

Ingredients

- 6 large eggs, hard-boiled, diced
- 1/4 C. diced red pepper
- 1/4 C. diced green pepper
- 1/2 C. mayonnaise
- 1 tbsp fresh lemon juice
- 2 tsps fresh snipped chives
- 2 tsps chopped fresh dill
- 1 tsp cider vinegar
- salt and pepper

Directions

- Get a large mixing bowl: Place in it the bell peppers with the chopped eggs.
- Get a small mixing bowl: Whisk in it the mayo, lemon juice, chives, dill and vinegar.
- Add the mayo sauce to the salad and toss them gently to combine. Adjust the seasoning of the salad then serve it.
- Enjoy.

Servings Per Recipe: 3

Timing Information:

Preparation	15 mins
Total Time	20 mins

Nutritional Information:

Calories	307.2
Fat	23.0g
Cholesterol	433.1mg
Sodium	11.9g
Carbohydrates	13.2g
Protein	307.2

* Percent Daily Values are based on a 2,000 calorie diet.

CHICKEN WITH WHITE GLAZE

Ingredients

- 2 C. meat, minced
- cayenne pepper, to taste
- 1 tbsp bell pepper, seeded and minced
- 1 egg, beaten with
- 1 tbsp water
- breadcrumbs

White Glaze

- 4 tbsps butter, melted
- 4 tbsps flour
- 1/2 tsp salt
- 1/8 tsp pepper
- 1 C. milk

Directions

- Get a mixing bowl: Mix in it the flour, melted butter, a pinch of salt and pepper.
- Pour the milk gradually into the mix while whisking all the time.
- Stir in the minced chicken with bell pepper and seasonings. Shape the mix into bite size pieces.
- Get a shallow dish: Whisk in it the egg with water. Dip the chicken meatballs in the egg and coat them with the breadcrumbs.
- Place a deep pan over medium heat. Heat in 1/4 inch of oil until it becomes hot. Cook in it the chicken bites until they become golden brown. Serve your chicken bites with your favorite dip.
- Enjoy.

Servings Per Recipe: 4

Timing Information:

Preparation	15 mins
Total Time	25 mins

Nutritional Information:

Calories	188.3
Fat	15.0g
Cholesterol	91.9mg
Sodium	9.0g
Carbohydrates	4.5g
Protein	188.3

* Percent Daily Values are based on a 2,000 calorie diet.

CHICAGO BURGERS WITH PEPPER AIOLI

Ingredients

- 3 stalks celery, diced
- 1 small onion, diced
- 1/4 C. low sodium soy sauce
- 2 tsps onion powder
- 2 tsps garlic powder
- 1/2 tsp ground black pepper
- 3 C. old fashioned oats
- 12 ounces mushrooms, finely chopped
- 1/2 C. whole wheat flour

Spicy Aoli

- 1/2 C. vegan mayonnaise
- 1/4 C. olive oil
- 1 jarred roasted red pepper, drained
- 1 garlic clove, minced

Directions

- Place a large saucepan over medium heat. Stir in it 4 C. water, celery, onion, soy sauce, onion powder, garlic powder, and pepper. Cook them until they start boiling.
- Lower the heat and cook them for an extra 6 min. Add the oats, mushrooms and flour. Let them cook for 6 min.
- Pour the mix into a large mixing bowl. Place it aside to cool down completely.
- Before you do anything else, preheat the oven to 350 F.
- Grease a cookie sheet with some butter. Divide the Veggie mix into 8 portions in the shape of patties.

- Place the patties on the cookie sheet and cook them for 16 min in the oven.
- Once the time is up, turn over the patties and cook them for 11 min. Allow the patties to lose heat completely.
- Before you do anything, preheat the grill.
- Cover the grill grates with a piece of foil and coat it with a cooking spray. Place the burgers over it and cook them for 8 min on each side.
- Get a food processor: Combine in it the pepper aioli and blend them smooth. Serve your burgers warm with the pepper aioli.
- Enjoy.

Servings Per Recipe: 8

Timing Information:

Preparation	0 mins
Total Time	50 mins

Nutritional Information:

Calories	260.1
Fat	12.0g
Cholesterol	3.6mg
Sodium	32.9g
Carbohydrates	7.1g
Protein	260.1

* Percent Daily Values are based on a 2,000 calorie diet.

ILLINOIS CHOWDER

Ingredients

- 2 lbs haddock, chunked
- 2 C. peeled and diced new potatoes
- 8 tbsps butter
- 1/4 C. chopped celery leaves
- 3 bay leaves
- 4 whole garlic cloves
- 2 1/2 tsps salt
- 1/4 tsp white pepper
- 1 clove garlic, minced
- 1 C. dry vermouth
- 2 C. boiling fish stock
- 2 C. half-and-half cream
- 1 1/2 tsps chopped fresh dill, topping

Directions

- Before you do anything, preheat the oven to 350 F.
- Place a large oven proof Dutch oven pot over medium heat. Stir in the butter with potato, fish, garlic, vermouth, a pinch of salt and pepper.
- Combine the celery leaves, bay leaves, and cloves in a piece of a cheesecloth seal it. Add it to the pot.
- Put on the lid and place the pot in the oven. Let it cook for 55 min.
- Once the time is up, drain the herbs bag and discard it. Stir in the boiling stock.
- Place a heavy saucepan over medium heat. Heat in it the half and half for 1 to 2 min without boiling it.
- Stir the half and half to the fish stew then serve it hot.
- Enjoy.

Servings Per Recipe: 6

Timing Information:

| Preparation | 20 mins |
| Total Time | 1 hr 20 mins |

Nutritional Information:

Calories	463.3
Fat	26.7g
Cholesterol	183.1mg
Sodium	1370.2mg
Carbohydrates	12.6g
Protein	42.0g

* Percent Daily Values are based on a 2,000 calorie diet.

Vanilla Cheesecakes

Ingredients

- 8 ounces cream cheese
- 1 egg
- 1 tsp vanilla
- 1/4 C. sugar
- 1 C. ground nuts
- 1/4 C. melted butter
- 3 tbsps sugar

Garnish

- cherry pie filling

Directions

- Before you do anything, preheat the oven to 375 F.
- Get a large mixing bowl: Combine in it the cream cheese with the egg, vanilla and 1/4 C. sugar. Beat them until they become smooth.
- Get a mixing bowl: Combine in it the ground nuts with the melted butter and 3 tbsps of sugar to make the crust mix.
- Grease 12 small cheesecake molds with some butter and press into them the nuts mix to make the crust.
- Pour the cream cheese mix over the crust. Place the mols on a cookie sheet and cook it in the oven for 15 min.
- Once the time is up, place the cheesecakes aside to cool down completely.
- loosen the molds around the cheesecakes and transfer them to a serving plate after they completely cool down.
- Serve your cheesecakes with your favorite toppings.
- Enjoy.

Servings Per Recipe: 12

Timing Information:

Preparation	20 mins
Total Time	1 hr

Nutritional Information:

Calories	122.6
Fat	9.4g
Cholesterol	43.1mg
Sodium	8.1g
Carbohydrates	1.6g
Protein	122.6

* Percent Daily Values are based on a 2,000 calorie diet.

Provolone Chicken Hoagies

Ingredients

- 8 chicken tenderloins
- 6 tbsps butter, softened
- 4 hoagie rolls, split
- 1/4 tsp oregano leaves
- 1/4 tsp fresh parsley, minced
- 12 slices hard salami
- provolone cheese, halved lengthwise
- 1/2 C. pizza sauce
- 1/3 C. mushroom, fresh, diced, sautéed
- 1/4 tbsp black olives, chopped

Directions

- Before you do anything, preheat the oven to 425 F.
- Lay the tenderloins on a lined up cookie sheet. Cook it in the oven for 6 min. Flip them and cook them for another 6 min.
- Smooth the butter over the rolls and top them with the minced parsley and oregano. Lay over them the salami and cheese slices with tenderloins.
- Drizzle the pizza sauce over them followed by the mushroom slices and olives.
- Serve your hoagies with some extra toppings of your choice.
- Enjoy.

Servings Per Recipe: 4

Timing Information:

| Preparation | 20 mins |
| Total Time | 30 mins |

Nutritional Information:

Calories	439.8
Fat	28.3g
Cholesterol	73.1mg
Sodium	1074.6mg
Carbohydrates	33.5g
Protein	12.5g

* Percent Daily Values are based on a 2,000 calorie diet.

ALTERNATIVE HOT DOGS CHICAGO STYLE

Ingredients

- 6 large leaves from one head romaine lettuce
- 6 turkey hot dogs
- 1/2 C. onion, Chopped fine
- 1/2 C. tomatoes, diced
- 1/2 C. pickle, diced
- 1/4 C. jalapeno, seeded and diced
- 4 tbsps Dijon mustard
- 3 ounces cheddar cheese
- celery seed, topping

Directions

- Place a large pan over medium heat. Grease it with a cooking spray. Place in it the hot dogs and cook them until they are browned on all sides.
- Get a small mixing bowl: Toss in it the onion with tomato, pickles, jalapeno, and a pinch of salt.
- Place a hot dog over a lettuce leave followed by 3/4 tbsp of mustard and 1/6 of the veggies mix. Sprinkle the cheese on top.
- Repeat the process with the remaining ingredients. Serve your hot dogs right away.
- Enjoy.

Servings Per Recipe: 6

Timing Information:

Preparation	10 mins
Total Time	15 mins

Nutritional Information:

Calories	181.7
Fat	14.8mg
Cholesterol	404.0mg
Sodium	24.1g
Carbohydrates	12.0g
Protein	181.7

* Percent Daily Values are based on a 2,000 calorie diet.

SIMPLE ITALIAN BEEF

Ingredients

- 10 lbs beef boneless round roast
- Worcestershire sauce
- garlic powder
- dried basil
- red pepper flakes
- water
- au jus sauce, next recipe

Directions

- Before you do anything, preheat the oven to 250 F.
- Coat the beef roast with Worcestershire sauce followed by garlic powder and dry basil one at a time.
- Season it with the red pepper flakes, some salt and pepper. Place it in a roasting pan. Cook it for 3 h 30 min.
- Drain the roast cover it completely with a piece of foil. Place it in the fridge to rest of at least 8 h.
- Thinly slice the roast and place it in zip lock bags then freeze them until ready to use.
- Enjoy.

Servings Per Recipe: 1

Timing Information:

Preparation	1 hr
Total Time	5 hrs

Nutritional Information:

Calories	0.0
Fat	0.0g
Cholesterol	0.0mg
Sodium	0.0mg
Carbohydrates	0.0g
Protein	0.0g

* Percent Daily Values are based on a 2,000 calorie diet.

How to Make Beef Au Jus (Roasted Beef Sauce)

Ingredients

- 1/4 C. beef fat drippings from roast beef
- 1 1/2 tbsps all-purpose flour
- 2 C. beef broth
- salt and ground black pepper to taste

Directions

- Get a frying hot then melt your fat in it. Combine in the flour with the fat and stir it completely. Continue stirring and heating until the mixture becomes thick for 4 mins.
- Add your broth to the pan then turn up the heat to high and get everything boiling completely.
- Continue to let the contents boil until it becomes a bit thicker then combine in your pepper and salt as needed.
- Enjoy.

Servings Per Recipe: 4

Timing Information:

Preparation	5 m
Cooking	10 m
Total Time	15 m

Nutritional Information:

Calories	53
Fat	1.1g
Carbohydrates	0g
Protein	17mg
Cholesterol	401mg
Sodium	2.3g

* Percent Daily Values are based on a 2,000 calorie diet.

Motel Pizza

Ingredients

- 2 C. all-purpose flour
- 1/2 C. warm water
- 1 tsp active dry yeast
- 1 tsp salt
- 1/3 C. corn oil
- 1 tsp pepper
- 1 tbsp dry oregano flakes
- 1 (14 ounce) cans diced tomatoes
- 12 ounces shredded mozzarella cheese

Directions

- Get a large mixing bowl: Stir in it 1 tsp salt with the yeast and warm water. let them sit for 6 min.
- Mix in 1/2 C. of flour. Combine in 3/4 flour and corn oil. Once again, mix in the remaining 3/4 C. flour.
- Place the dough on a floured surface and knead it for 6 min until it become soft.
- Place the dough in a greased bowl and lay a kitchen towel over it. Let it rest for 2 h.
- Once the time is up, knead the dough slightly then place it back in the bowl, cover it and let it rest for another 2 h.
- Before you do anything else, preheat the oven to 475 F.
- Transfer the dough to a floured working surface and roll it until it become 14 inches.
- Get a food processor: Place it in the tomato and purée it. Drizzle it all over the pizza crust. Top it with oregano, a pinch of salt and pepper.

- Lay over it your favorite toppings and top them with the mozzarella cheese.
- Cook the pizza in the oven for 14 min. Serve it hot.
- Enjoy.

Servings Per Recipe: 4

Timing Information:

Preparation	4 hrs
Total Time	4 hrs 10 mins

Nutritional Information:

Calories	628.8
Fat	32.6g
Cholesterol	54.5mg
Sodium	1116.6mg
Carbohydrates	55.2g
Protein	28.5g

* Percent Daily Values are based on a 2,000 calorie diet.

ILLINOIS SWEET SAVORY CHILI

Ingredients

- 2 lbs ground beef
- 1 C. yellow sweet onion
- 1 C. sweet bell pepper
- 2 stalks celery, diced
- 1 carrot, diced
- 2 jalapeno peppers, minced
- 2 (28 ounce) cans crushed tomatoes
- 1 (6 ounce) cans tomato paste
- 4 -8 garlic cloves, minced
- salt and pepper, to taste
- 2 ounces dark chocolate
- 1/8 C. orange juice
- 1/4 C. lime juice
- 1/4 C. lemon juice
- 1/2 tsp salt
- 1 tsp black pepper
- 1 tsp cayenne pepper
- 1 tsp cumin
- 1 tsp thyme
- 1 tsp basil
- 2 tsps oregano
- 1 tsp Hungarian paprika
- 2 tsps Mexican chili powder
- 2 tsps garlic powder
- 1 tsp onion powder
- 2 tsps dried parsley
- 1 tsp dried cilantro
- 1/2 C. brown sugar
- 1/2 C. unsweetened cocoa powder

Directions

- Get a mixing bowl: Mix in it all the spices including the cocoa powder and sugar.
- Place a Dutch oven over medium heat. Cook in it the beef for 8 min. Discard the excess fat. Season it with some salt and pepper.

- Push the browned meat to one side of the pot. Stir the onions, garlic, and jalapenos along with the remaining veggies on the other side of the pot.
- Let them cook for 5 min then sprinkle over them a pinch of salt and pepper.
- Add the tomato paste and mix them well. Stir in the crushed tomato followed by the spice mix. Cook them until they start simmering while stirring all the time.
- Add the Lemon juice, Lime juice and Orange juice with the chocolate pieces. Cook them until the chocolate melt while stirring all the time.
- Lower the heat and put on the lid. Cook the stew for 8 min. Serve it hot with some grated cheddar cheese.
- Enjoy.

Servings Per Recipe: 10

Timing Information:

Preparation	30 mins
Total Time	1 hr

Nutritional Information:

Calories	367.6
Fat	18.0g
Cholesterol	61.6mg
Sodium	549.2mg
Carbohydrates	36.1g
Protein	22.7g

* Percent Daily Values are based on a 2,000 calorie diet.

CLASSIC RITZ CHICKEN BAKE

Ingredients

- 4 boneless chicken breasts
- 1 package chopped broccoli, cooked
- 1 can corn
- 1 can cream of mushroom soup
- 1/4 C. milk
- 1/2 lb Velveeta cheese, diced
- 1/2 jar mushroom
- 1 jar pimiento
- Ritz crackers, crushed
- butter

Directions

- Bring a large pot of water to a boil. Cook in it the chicken breasts for 20 to 25 min or until they are done.
- Drain the chicken breasts and shred them.
- Before you do anything, preheat the oven to 450 F.
- Combine the shredded chicken, broccoli and corn in the greased baking dish.
- Place a heavy saucepan over medium heat. Combine in it the soup with milk, cheese, mushrooms and pimentos. Cook it for 4 min.
- Pour the mix all over the chicken and broccoli mix. Top it with the ritz crackers.
- Place the dish in the oven and cook it for 62 min. Serve it hot.
- Enjoy.

Servings Per Recipe: 8

Timing Information:

Preparation	45 mins
Total Time	1 hr 45 mins

Nutritional Information:

Calories	251.7
Fat	15.4g
Cholesterol	69.8mg
Sodium	737.5mg
Carbohydrates	6.6g
Protein	20.9g

* Percent Daily Values are based on a 2,000 calorie diet.

CLOUD GATE PIZZA SAUCE

Ingredients

- 1 (32 ounce) cans tomato puree
- 1 tsp oregano
- 1 tsp basil
- 1 tsp thyme
- 1 tsp marjoram
- 1 tsp garlic powder
- 1 tsp pepper
- salt (To taste)
- 1 tsp sugar

Directions

- Get a large mixing bowl: Combine in it all the ingredients and mix them well. Place them sauce in the fridge for 4 h.
- Use it for your pizzas, lasagna and other dish whenever you desire.
- Enjoy.

Servings Per Recipe: 2

Timing Information:

Preparation	2 mins
Total Time	2 mins

Nutritional Information:

Calories	190.0
Fat	1.0g
Cholesterol	0.0mg
Sodium	128.5mg
Carbohydrates	45.0g
Protein	7.9g

* Percent Daily Values are based on a 2,000 calorie diet.

Simple Vanilla Cookies

Ingredients

- 2 C. unsalted butter, at room temperature
- 1 1/2 C. sugar, plus extra for topping the cookies
- 1/4 tsp salt
- 3 1/2 C. all-purpose flour
- 2 tsps vanilla extract

Directions

- Before you do anything, preheat the oven to 350 F.
- Get a large mixing bowl: Beat in it the sugar with butter until they become light and smooth.
- Pour the sugar with salt into the bowl and mix them well.
- Add the flour gradually while mixing all the time until you get a smooth dough.
- Shape the dough into bite size pieces. Place them on a cookie sheet and cook them for 13 to 14 min or until they are golden brown.
- Enjoy.

Servings Per Recipe: 1

Timing Information:

| Preparation | 30 mins |
| Total Time | 42 mins |

Nutritional Information:

Calories	167.5
Fat	10.3g
Cholesterol	27.1mg
Sodium	17.8mg
Carbohydrates	17.6g
Protein	1.3g

* Percent Daily Values are based on a 2,000 calorie diet.

FRANKFURTER SALAD CHI-TOWN STYLE

Ingredients

- 1/4 C. yellow mustard
- 2 tbsps vinegar
- 1 tsp sugar
- 4 tbsps vegetable oil
- 1/2 medium red onion, thinly sliced
- 1 C. shredded cabbage
- 1 romaine lettuce hearts, shredded
- 2 tomatoes, diced
- 3 large garlic dill pickles, chopped
- celery salt
- black pepper
- 8 vienna beef hot dogs, sliced into 1-inch-thick slices on an angle

Directions

- Get a large mixing bowl: Whisk in it the mustard, vinegar, sugar, and about 3 tbsps of vegetable oil.
- Combine in the onions, cabbage, romaine, tomatoes, and pickles, celery salt and pepper then mix them well.
- Place a skillet over medium heat. Heat 1 tbsp of oil in it. Sauté in it the hot dog slices for 1 to 2 min on each side.
- Add the hot dog slices to the salad then serve it.
- Enjoy.

Servings Per Recipe: 4

Timing Information:

Preparation	10 mins
Total Time	15 mins

Nutritional Information:

Calories	491.8
Fat	41.1g
Cholesterol	47.7mg
Sodium	2400.1mg
Carbohydrates	19.1g
Protein	13.7g

* Percent Daily Values are based on a 2,000 calorie diet.

ALTERNATIVE DEEP DISH

Ingredients

Dough

- 1 C. warm tap water
- 1/4 ounce active dry yeast
- 3 1/2 C. flour
- 1/2 C. course ground cornmeal
- 1 tsp salt

Toppings

- 1 lb mozzarella cheese, sliced thin

- 1 lb Italian sausage, removed from the casing and crumbled
- 1 (14 1/2 ounce) cans diced tomatoes, drained
- 2 garlic cloves, peeled and minced
- 5 fresh basil leaves, chopped fine
- 4 tbsps grated parmesan cheese

Directions

- Get a large mixing bowl: Stir in the yeast with warm water.
- Pour 1 C. of flour, all of the cornmeal, salt, and vegetable oil in the same bowl. Combine them well. Add the remaining 1/2 C. of flour and mix them well.
- Place the dough in a greased bowl and cover it with a kitchen towel. Place it aside to rise for 1 h.
- Grease a 15 inches baking pan and press the pizza dough into it. Let it sit for 18 min.

- Before you do anything, preheat the oven to 500 F.
- Place a large skillet over medium heat. Cook in it the sausage for 8 min. Discard the excess fat.
- Score the pizza dough several times with a sharp knife. Spread the half of the mozzarella cheese over it followed by the cooked sausage, garlic and the remaining cheese.
- Lay the tomato slices on top followed by the parmesan cheese. Cook the pizza in the oven for 16 min.
- Lower the oven temperature to 400 F. Cook the pizza in it for an extra 30 min or until it is done to you liking. Serve it hot.
- Enjoy.

Servings Per Recipe: 8

Timing Information:

Preparation	2 hrs
Total Time	2 hrs 50 mins

Nutritional Information:

Calories	676.6
Fat	36.7g
Cholesterol	79.4mg
Sodium	1377.8mg
Carbohydrates	53.9g
Protein	31.5g

* Percent Daily Values are based on a 2,000 calorie diet.

COFFEE CAKES 101

Ingredients

- 1/2 C. margarine
- 1 (8 ounce) packages cream cheese
- 1 1/4 C. sugar
- 2 eggs
- 1 tsp vanilla extract
- 1 3/4 C. flour
- 1 tsp baking powder
- 1/2 tsp baking soda
- 1/4 C. milk

Coating

- 1/4 C. sugar
- 4 tbsps flour
- 4 tsps cinnamon
- 4 tbsps margarine

Directions

- Before you do anything, preheat the oven to 350 F.
- Get a large mixing bowl: Beat in it the margarine, cream cheese and sugar until they become light and smooth. Add the eggs with vanilla and beat them again.
- Get a mixing bowl: Stir in it the flour, baking powder and baking soda. Sift the mix over the cream mix with milk gradually while alternating between them and mixing all the time.
- Get a small mixing bowl: Mix in it the sugar, remaining flour, cinnamon and margarine until they become crumbly.
- Pour the batter into a greased baking pan. Sprinkle the sugar mix all over it.

- Place the cake in the oven and let it cook for 38 min. Allow it to cool down completely then serve it with your favorite toppings.
- Enjoy.

Servings Per Recipe: 12

Timing Information:

| Preparation | 10 mins |
| Total Time | 45 mins |

Nutritional Information:

Calories	323.5
Fat	15.2g
Cholesterol	52.5mg
Sodium	247.3mg
Carbohydrates	42.8g
Protein	4.6g

* Percent Daily Values are based on a 2,000 calorie diet.

CHICAGO TUNA SALAD

Ingredients

- 1/4 C. tomatoes, cubed
- 1/4 C. chopped dill pickle
- 2 tbsps chopped onions
- 1 tsp pickle
- celery salt (optional)
- 1 celery rib, chopped
- 1 tbsp mayonnaise
- 1 tbsp mustard
- 2 (5 ounce) cans light chunk tuna in water

Directions

- Get a large mixing bowl: Combine in it all the ingredients and toss them to coat.
- Place the salad in the fridge until ready to serve.
- Enjoy.

Servings Per Recipe: 8

Timing Information:

Preparation	1 min
Total Time	2 mins

Nutritional Information:

Calories	53.0
Fat	0.9g
Cholesterol	11.1mg
Sodium	215.4mg
Carbohydrates	1.3g
Protein	9.2g

* Percent Daily Values are based on a 2,000 calorie diet.

AMARETTO RAISINS COOKIES

Ingredients

- 1/2 C. raisins
- 1/2 C. chopped dates
- 1/3 C. amaretto di saronno liqueur
- 1/3 C. water
- 1 C. butter, softened
- 1 1/2 C. brown sugar
- 2 large eggs
- 1/2 tsp vanilla extract
- 1/2 tsp salt
- 1/4 tsp baking soda
- 2 C. flour
- 1/4 C. maple syrup
- 1/4 C. peanut butter
- 2 C. rolled oats
- 1/2 C. butterscotch chips
- 1/2 C. semi-sweet chocolate chips

Directions

- Get an airtight container: Combine in it the water with dates, raisins and amaretto. Let them soak for at least 24 hrs more.
- Get a large mixing bowl: Beat in it the butter with brown sugar until it become light and fluffy.
- Crack in it the eggs with vanilla and beat them again until they become smooth.
- Get another mixing bowl: Stir in it the salt, baking soda, and flour. Add them to the eggs mix and mix them well.
- Pour in the maple syrup with peanut butter and oats. Combine them well. Add the soaked raisins, dates and amaretto mix.

- Fold them into the dough along with the butterscotch and semi-sweet chocolate chips. Cover the dough with a plastic wrap and place it in the fridge for 1 h.
- Before you do anything else, preheat the oven to 350 F.
- Shape the dough medium sized balls and place them on lined up baking sheets with parchment paper.
- Cook the cookies in the oven for 18 to 22 min. Allow them to cool down completely then serve them.
- Enjoy.

Servings Per Recipe: 24

Timing Information:

Preparation	20 mins
Total Time	1 hr 20 mins

Nutritional Information:

Calories	269.7
Fat	12.0g
Cholesterol	37.9mg
Sodium	144.3mg
Carbohydrates	38.4g
Protein	3.8g

* Percent Daily Values are based on a 2,000 calorie diet.

GARLIC DOUGH FOR THIN CRUSTS

Ingredients

- 7 C. flour
- 1/2 tsp salt
- 1/2 C. olive oil
- 2 C. warm water
- 4 tsps yeast
- 12 ounces broth
- 8 -10 garlic cloves, very finely minced
- cornmeal, for rolling out

Directions

- Get a large mixing bowl: Stir in it the yeast with warm water and a pinch of salt.
- Add to them the oil with broth, garlic or basil and Parmesan cheese then mix them well.
- Add the flour gradually while mixing all the time until you get a smooth dough.
- Transfer the dough to a greased bowl and cover it with a kitchen towel. Place it aside to rest until it doubles in size.
- Before you do anything, preheat the oven to 500 F.
- Place the dough on a floured surface and roll it until it becomes 1/8 inch thick.
- Pierce the pizza dough several times with a fork then cook it in the oven for 6 to 8 min or until it become golden.
- Serve your pizza crust with your favorite toppings.
- Enjoy.

Servings Per Recipe: 10

Timing Information:

Preparation	2 hrs
Total Time	2 hrs 10 mins

Nutritional Information:

Calories	434.5
Fat	11.7g
Cholesterol	0.0mg
Sodium	121.9mg
Carbohydrates	68.7g
Protein	9.8g

* Percent Daily Values are based on a 2,000 calorie diet.

Homemade Deep Dish

Ingredients

Midwestern Filling

- 1 bunch spinach, washed, stems removed, and lightly wilted
- 8 ounces shredded mozzarella cheese
- 2 ounces Canadian bacon, slices diced
- 1 tsp oregano
- 2 garlic cloves, sliced thinly
- 2 ounces mushrooms, sliced
- 2 C. buffalo
- 2 C. moose, or hamburger

Simpler Filling

- 8 ounces shredded mozzarella cheese
- 1/4 C. shredded parmesan cheese
- 1/4 lb hot Italian sausage, crumbled
- 1/3 C. pepperoni, pieces
- 1/4 C. sliced black olives
- 1/4 C. sliced green olives
- 5 ounces frozen chopped spinach
- 1 tsp oregano
- 1 tbsp chopped parsley
- 2 C. buffalo, or ground chuck

Directions

- Before you do anything, preheat the oven to 450 F.
- Roll the pizza dough that you are using on a floured surface. Press half of it into the bottom of a 14 inches baking pan.
- Cook the pizza crust in the oven for 3 to 4 min.

- Get a large mixing bowl: Combine in it the spinach, cheese, Canadian bacon, oregano, garlic, buffalo meat, moose meat and mushrooms.
- Pour the mix all over the baked pizza crust. Lay over it the second pizza crust and press the edges to seal it.
- Place the pizza pan in the oven and cook it for 48 min. Allow the pizza pan to lose heat for 6 min then serve it with your favorite toppings.
- Enjoy.

Servings Per Recipe: 1

Timing Information:

Preparation	34 mins
Total Time	57 mins

Nutritional Information:

Calories	2179.9
Fat	150.3g
Cholesterol	475.6mg
Sodium	6773.2mg
Carbohydrates	50.9g
Protein	164.0g

* Percent Daily Values are based on a 2,000 calorie diet.

BLUE SIRLOIN STEAK

Ingredients

- 4 sirloin steaks

Marinade

- Worcestershire sauce
- soy sauce
- cooking sherry
- red wine vinegar

Flavored Butter

- 2 tbsps butter, softened
- 2 tbsps blue cheese, crumbled
- 2 -3 green onions, finely chopped

Directions

- Get a large zip lock bag: Place it in the sirloin steaks with a splash of Worcestershire sauce, soy sauce, cooking sherry and red wine vinegar.
- Seal the bag and place it aside to sit for 35 min.
- Before you do anything else, preheat the grill.
- Drain the steaks and cook them on the grill after greasing it for 5 to 6 min on each side.
- Get a small mixing bowl: Combine in it the butter, cheese and onion.
- Serve your grilled steaks warm with the blue cheese butter.
- Enjoy.

Servings Per Recipe: 4

Timing Information:

Preparation	10 mins
Total Time	20 mins

Nutritional Information:

Calories	1290.2
Fat	84.2g
Cholesterol	474.4mg
Sodium	426.9mg
Carbohydrates	0.6g
Protein	124.5g

* Percent Daily Values are based on a 2,000 calorie diet.

Simple Garlic Pizza Crust

Ingredients

- 1 (1/4 ounce) package active dry yeast
- 1 1/4 C. lukewarm water
- 3 1/4 C. flour, plus more for dusting
- 1 tsp sugar
- 1/2 C. cornmeal
- 1 tsp salt
- 4 tbsps unsalted butter, melted
- 1 garlic clove, ground to a paste
- pizza toppings, your choice

Directions

- Get a large mixing bowl: Stir in the warm water with yeast and stir them.
- Pour in 1/4 C. flour with sugar and mix them well. Add the rest of the warm water, 3 C. flour, the cornmeal and salt. Mix them well.
- Add the butter with garlic and mix them well until you get a smooth dough.
- Place the dough on a floured surface and knead it for at least 14 min until it become soft.
- Get a large mixing bowl: Grease it with some olive oil and place the dough ball in it. Cover the dough with a plastic wrap and let it rest for 1 h.
- Knead the dough again for at least 2 min. Press it into the bottom of a greased baking pan. Let it rest for 22 min.
- Lay over it your favorite toppings and bake it to your liking.

Servings Per Recipe: 6

Timing Information:

| Preparation | 1 hr 40 mins |
| Total Time | 2 hrs 10 mins |

Nutritional Information:

Calories	358.0
Fat	8.7g
Cholesterol	20.3mg
Sodium	395.2mg
Carbohydrates	60.8g
Protein	8.3g

* Percent Daily Values are based on a 2,000 calorie diet.

ITALIAN STYLE GRILLED CHICKEN

Ingredients

- 5 -6 chicken parts, thighs
- 1/2 C. mild yellow mustard
- 1 C. Italian dressing
- 1/4 C. light brown sugar
- 2 -3 tbsps Lawry's Seasoned Salt
- 2 -3 tbsps black pepper
- 1/4 C. paprika

Directions

- Before you do anything, preheat the grill and grease it.
- Get a large mixing bowl: Combine all the ingredients except for the chicken to make the rub.
- Add the chicken pieces and toss them to coat.
- Grill the chicken pieces for 10 to 15 min on each side or until they are done to your liking. Serve them warm.
- Enjoy.

Servings Per Recipe: 5

Timing Information:

Preparation	15 mins
Total Time	50 mins

Nutritional Information:

Calories	337.0
Fat	21.9g
Cholesterol	44.0mg
Sodium	809.4mg
Carbohydrates	21.7g
Protein	15.9g

* Percent Daily Values are based on a 2,000 calorie diet.

Downtown Ribs

Ingredients

- 2 full baby back rib racks

Dry Rub

- 1 tbsp dried mustard
- 1 tbsp paprika
- 1 tbsp dark brown sugar
- 1 1/2 tsps garlic powder
- 1 1/2 tsps onion powder
- 1 tsp cayenne pepper
- 1 1/2 tsps celery salt
- 1/2 tsp ground allspice

Wood Chips & BBQ Sauce

- 1 C. hickory chips, soaking in water for 15 min
- reserved 2 tbsp dry rub seasonings
- 1 1/4 C. ketchup
- 1/4 C. molasses
- 1/4 C. cider vinegar
- 1/4 C. water
- 1/8 tbsp liquid smoke

Directions

- Remove the membrane on the backside of the ribs.
- Get a mixing bowl: Mix it the rub mix. Rub the mix into the rubs with your hands.
- Drain the wood chips and place them in a roasting pan. Put it in the main side of the grill and heat it on high. Place another pan full of water beside it.
- Let the grill heat for 15 min the turn off the medium flame and high one to medium.

- Place the ribs on the grill after greasing it. Put on the lid and cook them for 48 min.
- In the meantime, preheat the oven to 250 F.
- Fill a roasting pan with water and top it with a wiring rack. Place the rib slabs over it and wrap a large piece of foil around them with the pan.
- Cook them in the oven for 2 h. Turn off the heat and let them rest for 12 min.
- Get a small mixing bowl: Whisk in it the spice rub, ketchup, molasses, cider vinegar, water, liquid smoke to make barbecue sauce.
- Serve the ribs with the sauce.
- Enjoy.

Servings Per Recipe: 4

Timing Information:

Preparation	30 mins
Total Time	3 hrs 30 mins

Nutritional Information:

Calories	176.7
Fat	1.4g
Cholesterol	0.0mg
Sodium	847.4mg
Carbohydrates	41.9g
Protein	2.5g

* Percent Daily Values are based on a 2,000 calorie diet.

HOW TO MAKE SAUSAGES

Ingredients

- 1 1/2 tsps salt
- 3 1/2 tsps paprika
- 2/3 tsp garlic powder
- 2/3 tsp fennel seed
- 1 tsp ground black pepper
- 1/4 tsp red pepper flakes
- 1/2 tsp oregano
- 1/2 tsp sage
- 1/2 tsp basil
- 1/2 tsp thyme
- 1 lb ground lean beef

Directions

- Get a large mixing bowl: Place in it the minced beef.
- Get a small mixing bowl: Combine in it the remaining ingredients well. Add it to the minced beef and mix them well.
- Wrap the mix in a piece of a plastic wrap and put it in the fridge for an overnight to soak the flavors. Use your sausage as you desire.
- Enjoy.

Servings Per Recipe: 3

Timing Information:

Preparation	15 mins
Total Time	15 mins

Nutritional Information:

Calories	412.7
Fat	32.5g
Cholesterol	109.0mg
Sodium	1250.4mg
Carbohydrates	2.8g
Protein	26.2g-

* Percent Daily Values are based on a 2,000 calorie diet.

THANKS FOR READING! JOIN THE CLUB AND KEEP ON COOKING WITH 6 MORE COOKBOOKS....

http://bit.ly/1TdrStv

 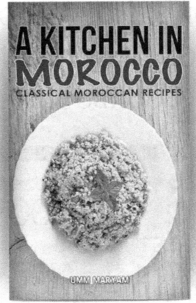 

To grab the box sets simply follow the link mentioned above, or tap one of book covers.

This will take you to a page where you can simply enter your email address and a PDF version of the box sets will be emailed to you.

Hope you are ready for some serious cooking!

http://bit.ly/1TdrStv

COME ON...
LET'S BE FRIENDS :)

We adore our readers and love connecting with them socially.

Like BookSumo on Facebook and let's get social!

Facebook

And also check out the BookSumo Cooking Blog.

Food Lover Blog

CPSIA information can be obtained
at www.ICGtesting.com
Printed in the USA
BVHW01s2156241018
531173BV00004B/42/P